How To Help Your Child Succeed On The SAT/ACT

The Ultimate Guide for Parents to SAT/ACT Success

Mark Richman

iUniverse, Inc.
Bloomington

How To Help Your Child Succeed On The SAT/ACT
The Ultimate Guide for Parents to SAT/ACT Success

iUniverse books may be ordered through booksellers or by contacting:

iUniverse
1663 Liberty Drive
Bloomington, IN 47403
www.iuniverse.com
1-800-Authors (1-800-288-4677)

ISBN: 978-1-4759-5051-9 (sc)
ISBN: 978-1-4759-5052-6 (ebk)

Library of Congress Control Number: 2012917105

Printed in the United States of America

iUniverse rev. date: 01/02/2013

HOW TO HELP
YOUR CHILD SUCCEED ON
THE SAT/ACT

Drawing of Me

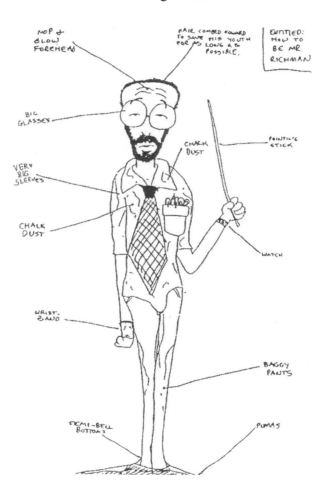

Contents

Your Child Can Survive and Thrive on the SAT and ACT Exams

"How To Help Your Child Succeed on the SAT and ACT" will serve as your road map to ease you along the often bumpy, unpaved and pothole - filled highway to successful results on these important College entrance exams.

This book has helped thousands of parents greatly improve the SAT and ACT Exam results of their children. It can help you and your children as well.

Discover how easy it is to:

-Increase Scores In All SAT/ACT Exam Areas: Math, Grammar, Writing, Vocabulary, Reading Comprehension, Essay Writing, and Science. Through a unique combination of strategies, guidance, suggestions, networking, using both new as well as traditional techniques, your children will become motivated to study and will even look forward to their exam prep. They will be provided with opportunities for positive outcomes and the building of confidence in a framework of success and excitement.

- Manage Their Study Time and Preparation. Mr. Richman will supply you with a blueprint for successful exam preparation via a structured system of procedures that will answer nearly all of your SAT/ACT preparation questions and will cover nearly every situation that could arise in this critical exam planning.

-Build Pupil Self-Esteem. This book will help you gain the insight necessary to aid your children in increasing their self-esteem, so critically important to their personality development and exam success.

Introduction

You're getting ready for college. The SAT or ACT is now on your radar screen. What to do? This book, authored by a veteran teacher and SAT/ACT tutor, will serve as your roadmap to help you navigate through the potentially confusing set of problems that many encounter in their "how do we best prepare" mindset. Remember, we will be discussing the SAT and the ACT. Nearly all colleges accept both exams.

Many go in to take the PSAT ("Practice" SAT) in grade ten knowing next to nothing about the SAT and ACT. This book will give you ideas on how to best prepare for these exams. It will suggest wonderful resources with which to consult from the literally hundreds of books out there. This book will put the test in perspective. It will expose you to the ideas, suggestions, thoughts, feelings, fears and experiences of current seniors who've already been through the whole process as well as the sophomores and juniors who are set to take the journey or who are already on the trip.

There absolutely are strategies and methods that one can and should follow in order to prep for the SAT or ACT, two of the most important tests in one's academic life. We will show you how to maximize your potential, reduce your anxiety, enjoy learning, improve your mathematics, your writing, reading, and oral presentation skills. You are in a very exciting period of your life and we will help guide you through it!

This book, by a (very) veteran educator, will provide you with unique insight not appearing in most other SAT/ACT Prep Manuals.

Although mainly for parents (and most of the dialogue is directed to them), it can be helpful to teachers, students and tutors as well.

Chapter One

About the Author

Mark Richman has been teaching for over 38 years. He worked thirty - one of those years in the NYC School System. His first twenty years in NYC were served on the middle school level at JHS 43 (nineteen there and one at JHS 62), in Brooklyn, where he performed as a math teacher and as Dean of Discipline. He then taught for 5 years at Brooklyn's Lincoln High School. He not only taught math to pupils in grades 9 through 12 (Algebra, Geometry and Trigonometry), but he also taught "AP Calculus" for three years. At Lincoln he served as the union "Chapter Leader" of his school.

In 1997 (after being in the classroom for 24 years), he moved into administration where he served at Brooklyn's Erasmus Hall HS as the supervisor of math, guidance, organization and security.

The following year, he moved into "staff and curriculum development" for many of the High Schools of Brooklyn and Staten Island in NYC. In this role, he had the wonderful opportunity to train teachers in the improvement of their craft. After serving in this role for three years, he again returned to the classroom where he became a math teacher at Automotive High School in Brooklyn, NY. He again taught math to many High School pupils at this vocational school.

The following year he was called upon to serve once again in administration at The High School of Economics and Finance in Manhattan (right across from the World Trade Center). As described in some detail later in the book, his third day on the job was 9/11/01.

In Sept. of 2002, he returned to the classroom for two more years (in NYC) at Port Richmond HS in Staten Island, NY - another tough inner city school. In June of 2004, he retired from NYC after 31 years and is now (November 2012) in his ninth year as a teacher at Columbia HS in Maplewood New Jersey.

These many experiences in education are discussed in this book and serve as the groundwork for many of the insights that Mr. Richman relates to his readers.

In the Appendix, there is an extensive summary of Mr. Richman's career and his Educational Philosophy. Reading it will help to understand much of his SAT/ACT insights and philosophy.

Chapter Two

Why I Wrote This Book

Every year a new crop of pupils begins the college entrance "process". There are the interviews, the tours, the financial aid, the applications, the anxieties and, of course, the "SAT/ACT." The large majority of pupils entering the eleventh grade truly know very little about these exams: what is on them, how to prepare for them, how to improve their scores, which ones to take and when to take them. This book is intended to ease pupils into this often confusing process and give them confidence that they will get through it all - and, likely, quite successfully.

Students will learn about the test calendars, scheduling, planning, preparing, critical resources, and insight into the different types of exams and options possible.

Pupils and parents (and even teachers and tutors) of any school - age child will find this information helpful. Even parents of younger children can benefit. But as pupils enter grades eight through twelve, the need for this material grows exponentially. And it is truly the "rising" high school juniors (summer of the upcoming junior year) who critically need knowledge in this arena.

In my discussion involving pupil commentary we will see that most pupils are quite unaware of the impending "ordeal." Yet after it's over, most find that it was not as big a deal as it had been billed to be. As in most endeavors in life it is often quite beneficial (from almost every angle imaginable) to get familiar with "ropes" of a process - in this case, of course, the SAT/ACT "megilla."

When pupils become familiar with the entire SAT/ACT situation and its logistics from A to Z, much of the complications, difficulties and anxieties are diminished. That is one of the major purposes of this book - to ease and guide pupils through the (mostly) eleventh grade "rite of passage" known as the SAT/ACT.

The process can even become "fun" for the pupil. In addition to improving their SAT/ACT score this process (reflected in the content of this book) will also help them become better students, become more organized, improve vocabulary, reading comprehension, and mathematics and study skills. Along with enhanced vocabulary and self-confidence, speaking and listening skills will also improve. Pupils will gain confidence in these types of standardized exams that they will be confronting from time to time in their future. For example, they shall go through similar preps in their graduate school application process, on their upcoming college freshman placement exams as well as on the usual tests along their continuous educational journey. This book will teach them those all important "ropes" that make success in any new adventure that much easier and less stressful. The books that they will use for their review, the help that they may need to receive (from tutors, classes, guidance personnel, self-study methodology, and relaxation strategies) are all discussed in this book that will positively enhance their experience with this "rite of (SAT/ACT) passage." The book will teach pupils major score - enhancement strategies whether their "starting point" baseline results are low or high. Using this book will greatly increase probability of score growth.

As far as psychology and its impact on exam results: I worked with a so - called "rising" senior during the summer before twelfth grade. She had taken the SAT once as a junior and did not do that well! She was down on herself, became quite negative, lost self confidence and was very "stressed out." She had not prepared at all for the SAT and knew very little about the ACT.

Strategy. Insight. Planning. More reasons why I wrote this book. First of all she should have prepared for the 11th grade SAT. She likely would have done better, allowing for stress relief early in the college application process. However, now that she discovered the ACT and began practicing for it, she started gaining confidence again. She scheduled herself for the September ACT in order not to have to wait for the late October ACT. This way she would be able to apply for early admission if necessary. But more importantly, she did very well, thus having good scores "in the bank," relieving loads of pressure. The ACT was "her exam."

These last two paragraphs show you more of what reading this book can do for pupils. It makes them aware of test calendars, scheduling, planning, preparing, knowledge of access to critical resources and insight into the different types of exams and options possible.

When I was a first year teacher, a first year camp counselor, a first year assistant principal, or a first year union leader it was always that A to Z orientation (or "ropes") that eased my bumpy ride and greatly shortened the "learning curve."

Similarly, it is this book (and one reason why I wrote it) that will give students that quick (relatively) orientation so critical to exam success.

What qualifies me to write this book? Teaching for 38 years, tutoring for 25 and serving as a staff developer, helped provide me with in depth knowledge of the learning process and of methods to assist pupils in succeeding on "high stakes" exams. In addition, as an Assistant Principal of Guidance and as a veteran camp counselor, I received great insight into the influence of psychology on the learning process. It is often more than knowledge that goes into exam success here. We have many other factors at work too. We have motivation, support, methodology and planning, we have influences from parents, teachers and friends. Just take a look at the Circle of Success (in Appendix and detailed later in the book) to see what goes into our expected positive outcome! My experiences in education and beyond eminently qualify me as an expert in this field. My track record in working with students is getting better every year as I gather more knowledge and analytic evidence from my involvement with the exams.

As the SAT changed in 2005 and will continue to change well into the future, the teaching strategies must also adapt and change. It is very interesting and challenging to be involved with this ongoing process. So many young lives are positively affected by these wonderful explorations.

That all being said, many students will take the SAT/ACT journey nearly "solo." They may not have a tutor or never attend any classes. Reading this book is the perfect "flight plan" for their upcoming long and sometimes bumpy journey. Thus no matter which route they take to achieve their dream SAT/ACT score, this book will guide them every step of the way!

Again the material in this "guide" is for both pupils and parents. Both can derive major benefit and if these two "constituencies" work together as a team, results will be even greater!

Chapter Three

Beginnings

SAT/ACT. Your ticket to college. As many know (by now) the SAT consists of three sections - Math, Verbal (vocabulary and reading comprehension) and "Writing" (two parts here - 70% multiple choice on grammar rules and 30% on essay writing). It seems that many colleges put much of their SAT/ACT - influenced admission decisions on the math and critical reading parts of the exam. However, colleges can, in addition, see the actual essay that the candidate composed. The pupils now have to write their pieces completely on their own under lots of time pressure. In other words, poor writers will now be exposed. The twenty - five minute SAT essay (and 30 - minute ACT essay) will give colleges an opportunity to view the pupils' writings. Previously, this was not possible. As more and more weight is given to the Writing section by college admissions committees, success on this section will become more critical.

It is important that the pupil obtain some sort of "baseline" figure that is fairly accurate. You need to know "where you're at" as far as planning and SAT Prep procedures. In other words, for example, when I first begin tutoring or advising a student, I ask for a set of scores. This is incredibly helpful. Many times the pupil has no scores so I advise the parent to "go out and get some." What does this mean?

Pupils begin SAT/ACT prep at different stages of their careers. The earlier the better! I always advise tenth and eleventh graders to take the PSAT in the fall of that respective school year. The scores are pretty accurate and give an idea of pupil status as of that point. The PSAT is quite a bit shorter than the real SAT and doesn't contain an essay but it does give a somewhat accurate current status report. Remember, in our book we shall cover all information regarding the SAT and ACT. So hang in there!!

Some schools invite SAT exam prep companies like Kaplan or Princeton Review into the school to administer a full length SAT Practice test, usually on a Saturday morning.

Preparation for the SAT can be tedious. It may take hours of practice, hours of memorization, and at times hours of frustration. Unfortunately, for college bound juniors, seniors, and even sophomores, you have no choice. Keeping in mind that the SAT may not be a fun adventure, you should know that this doesn't mean it has to be unnecessarily difficult. If you manage your time properly and put your effort to good use, you will see the results you deserve. In fact, your prep time may even become fun for you - something you truly look forward to. I had one pupil who took his practice questions as true challenges and as he got better, the questions became more and more "game - like" and challenging. In fact, he began doing SAT math questions for relaxation - he even saw it as more fun than watching TV or using his computer. And his results (especially in math) skyrocketed from previous exams with the result that he gained admission to his first choice college.

Before you begin preparing, there are a few preliminary steps you should take. First of all, as mentioned, if your school offers the PSAT, you should definitely take it as a sophomore and as a junior. Even though you can only qualify for national merit recognition as a junior, you can still learn approximately "where you stand" in terms of the SAT as a sophomore. The PSAT is a good precursor exam and if you know early on where your faults lie, it will be easier to correct them and work on them.

We said you need a good baseline status reading. Thus, let's talk about the PSAT vs. the Kaplan or Princeton Review prep test. All are good prep exams but there are differences. The PSAT is a much shorter SAT. It doesn't give you the total experience of a full - length complete SAT exam. There are not as many sections and there is no essay. However its scores give the pupil an early and rather accurate indication of his current ability. It (the PSAT) is also given under secure and realistic test conditions. When your score comes back, it is accompanied by a full report including the actual questions and your answers. You can truly analyze your results thoroughly. You can see which questions you got wrong and why you got them wrong. You can analyze your answer patterns and gain a great baseline of your approximate status.

Companies such as Kaplan and Princeton Review often have full length SAT practice tests available. As we said, some schools have Kaplan, e.g., come in and administer the exam to pupils on a Saturday. It is fully proctored by representatives from Kaplan and from the school. If your school doesn't have this service, you can call the various companies and arrange to take the test, often at the company's site. These tests are quite realistic, both in time and predictability. They include essays with full reports and analyses. I find them to be quite reliable as to pupil ability at the given time that the test is taken.

Another option is administering the exam to you using one of the test prep books. The problem with this strategy is that it lacks the realism that can only be present when an exam is proctored at a realistic test site.

So, by taking a diagnostic exam, you will see where your strengths and weaknesses lie before you engage in any practice or have done very little studying. This will help maximize time spent on the subject matter you need to learn and minimize relearning topics you already know well.

Let's say, e.g., that your PSAT or Kaplan scores come back with critical reading at 620, writing/grammar at 460, and math at 490, with an essay reading of 6 (3 + 3) - [more about essay scoring later]. Of course any permutation of scores will come in depending on the individual pupil in question. If scores come in as above, I would naturally go to work on grammar, which, as we'll discuss, with study, usually increases most easily of all the scores. We would work on the essay to get that score up. I'd feel pretty confident about the reading section although reading strategies and vocabulary building should raise that score. Math can be difficult to move but with the proper practice with careful analysis, that score should rise as well. Remember, all pupils are completely unique in ability and in learning style and improvement programs must fit the pupil like a perfectly tailored glove (one reason why one on one instruction, whenever possible, is best).

When you decide to begin your SAT/ACT Prep, a decision must also be made as to your method of preparation. Three major options exist for students. First, there is the large group method. In this choice, you sign up for an SAT class consisting of a group of pupils, ranging in size from two or three to as many as 20 or 25. Major exam prep companies (such as Kaplan and Princeton Review), as well as others, offer these classes. The problem here is that the pupil often needs to sit through long sessions often filled with questions from others which may or may not pertain to the pupil's specific needs. It is nearly impossible to receive the tailored instruction that one often requires. Although the hourly fee is usually less than it would be for a private tutor, pupils simply do not receive the individual attention and instruction that they need and deserve.

An alternative approach wherein often this problem is solved is one-on-one private tutoring. In this way, the pupil can truly secure personalized attention tailor - made to his individual needs. The instructor can check homework and develop a wonderful academic relationship with the pupil. At one point several years ago, I conducted small SAT classes - usually consisting of between 2 and 6 pupils in a class. I found that it was quite ineffective. Pupils often daydreamed, and I needed to lecture often. I was truly unable to zero in on their individual learning styles, to religiously check their assignments and to "get into their thought processes," which I am easily able to do in a one on one situation. So if you choose to use a tutor, one - on - one tutoring is usually the best! Unfortunately, the costs of one-on-one tutoring can be high and financial considerations are always relevant.

Finally, there is the "go it on your own" prep method. Of course, this is essentially a misnomer, as there are the many support materials at one's disposal. Examples include the Princeton Review books, Kaplan books, and College Board workbooks, as well as all others that will be mentioned in this book. If pupils use these support materials and work diligently with them, the results can also be similarly positive. Again, pupils may need to reach out to teachers or other support people for explanations or guidance with very difficult questions or other miscellaneous advice.

What prep information should you take with you from this section? Let's recap some of the highlights: Any one - on - one prep session, although usually more costly, far outweighs the "class" setups. With one on one, pupils get much more attention and instruction molded to their unique needs! However, the same principles that apply to one on one tutoring are also applicable to the pupil who is prepping mostly on her own. She should focus on her own areas of strength and weakness and tailor her prep work to these strengths and weaknesses.

Much work, no matter how one chooses to prepare, is done by pupils on their own. The tutor or class instructor (or no tutor if you choose to go at it alone) will assign to you loads of practice problems (based on material learned) found in the many suggested publications. Practice must be done rigorously, analytically, and responsibly by the pupil. Often teacher (or tutor) support (or that by friend or relative) is necessary on an ongoing basis to help guide the pupil in his studies and help to explain confusing questions.

It's never too early to begin your SAT/ACT prep and summer is always a superb time as there is little interference from the coursework and pressures that usually begin in Sept and don't stop until June. There are certain specific procedures to follow, as we've seen, and will see, for each section and subsection.

Preparation for all but the (the Einsteins) very few is essential. With lots of practice, concentration, a positive attitude and with the suggestions set forth in this book, SAT/ACT scores can increase dramatically over time. Begin your prep early and do it responsibly and ultimately you'll be very happy with your results!

Your strengths and weaknesses may surprise you. You can always improve your score, so don't feel trapped or frustrated. The grammar section, as mentioned, is usually the easiest to improve mainly because students aren't often taught grammar rules in school. After reading a grammar book (like the soon to be discussed "Barrons"), then learning and practicing the grammar rules, the scores for students usually increase dramatically. As we will see, pupils do not just read a grammar book. They study the relevant rules, practice them and back them up with more support from other books (we shall discuss) like "Holt's English Workshop."

The critical reading and math sections often take more work to improve, but your score can absolutely increase if you're willing to put in the necessary time. Once again, the purpose of this manual is to introduce the pupil (and his parent) to the "ins and outs" of SAT/ACT Prep. It is written by me, Mark Richman, who, for over 37 years, has been teaching and tutoring pupils preparing for the SAT and ACT. I have witnessed the change in the SAT and have kept up with the latest strategies for SAT/ACT Test Prep. I will recommend methods of preparation, what to expect on the exams and escort you along the test prep route, as well as guide you to many of the available support materials. In fact, I provide you with my e-mail address, Richteach3@ aol.com (here in fall 2012) so that you can contact me with questions that might arise from reading my manual.

It is important that you get to know the SAT and ACT. Just as you would want to know at least a little information about a person before a blind date, you definitely would want to know enough about the SAT or ACT to feel comfortable approaching either exam. You need to know the rules of the SAT or ACT, the breakdown of the times (minutes) per section, and some general ideas about the question types and answer options. The grueling exams can be exhausting, but if you are prepared and know the exam inside and out, you will feel more confident. In order to get to know the SAT/ACT better, you will want to get a free SAT/ACT Prep Booklet from your school's guidance office and read the entire pamphlet. You can also purchase, e.g., the soon to be discussed College Board's "The Official SAT Study Guide." Both of these College Board sponsored books will help you learn the ins and outs of the SAT and give you an overview of the entire test. Similar prep books are available for the ACT and the SAT II's.

Once you've taken a diagnostic test and/or the PSAT and know the rules, regulations, and expectations of the SAT/ACT, you can begin to maximize your study. While many students don't begin preparing for the SAT/ACT until the junior or even as late as the summer before the senior year (very late), for the highest score possible, it doesn't hurt to start in 9th or 10th grade. It is never too early to begin learning SAT words and practicing concepts and strategies that will help you on the exams. Remember, the exams are long and can be both mentally and physically grueling. By beginning preparation as early as possible, you will be more in shape and ready for the test. What do we mean by being "in shape" for the test? Well what we mean is in shape both physically and mentally. The exam can be that grueling 3.5 to 4 hour marathon. Often analysis reveals that success in answering questions often tails off as the test proceeds. This may not be because of question difficulty necessarily, but often is because the pupil just gets tired as the test proceeds and pupil concentration, focus and accuracy wane. When pupils are strong and in shape both physically and mentally, these problems will often cease.

The most effective study strategy is simple, but also most undesirable by many students: practice. By just taking the SAT or ACT once, your score will likely improve the second time around. Most agree that just taking the exams will improve your result. The reason is simply the fact that the pupil experiences all that there is to experience when taking the exam once. Much of the tension, anxiety and stress are removed by this first exam experience. Again nearly all that I write about the SAT applies equally well to the ACT. If it doesn't, I will indicate the difference where appropriate.

Practice on the questions and analysis of your answers are the best sure - fire strategies to make improvements. As we will indicate often in our book, practice is the best way to improve your score but practice must be accompanied by this careful analysis. This means that for each question you need to know reasons why your answer is correct and often it helps to know why the other choices are wrong. Without this critical analysis, scores won't improve nearly as much. That's why one needs practice materials containing answers fully worked out in detail (with wrong answers explained), and/ or one often needs a tutor or reference person to explain questions that are ambiguous.

Chapter Four

Supports and Tips

The support books are an essential ingredient to your test prep procedure. These books can provide you with the knowledge, skills and practice materials necessary for SAT/ACT success. To guide you with your preparation, these are some of the large number of books you may want to invest in to help you:

College Board's "The Official SAT Study Guide"

The College Board. The Official SAT Study Guide. First and Second Editions. New York: College Board, 2005 - 2011. Print.

Let's discuss this "Big Blue" book, as we shall call it. We shall refer to it often. "Big Blue" is a great text that contains wonderful data on the ins and outs of the exam. It also contains 8 full length practice tests that are great review for the SAT. It does contain the answers to these 8 exams, but doesn't explain the answers - a big problem. What the book does have is an accompanying "virtual text" called the SAT "Online Course" (which does indeed have full explanations). Available from the College Board, "Big Blue" is sold mainly from the College Board web - site: www.collegeboard.com. By the way, this site is a superb resource for day to day (keeps you up to date about the SAT) info on the exam and prepping for it. The current cost for the online course (Fall 2012) is about $50 (with purchase of "Big Blue"). Purchasing the online course gives you one year of access to it. What it contains are answers to every single question on all 8 of the "Big Blue" exams. Not only answers but full explanations, quite well - done. It explains why all the wrong answers are wrong. In addition, it provides additional practice exams with the same full explanations. One can print out the data on paper or view it online. One can also take these exams online and they are automatically graded. In addition each exam contains one essay. With the online course pupils can print out model answers to the essay that truly help them in their essay preparation techniques.

Barron's SAT II - Writing

Ehrenhaft, George. Fourth Edition. Hauppauge NY: Barron's Educational Series, 2004. Print.
This book is a superb publication for the grammar/writing section both on the SAT and ACT. You can still order it on the internet or order its successor. It covers everything you need to help you prep for the grammar/writing section. More about it in the grammar section.

Holt's English Workshop -

English Workshop: Complete Course. New York: 1995. Print. ISBN 0 - 03 - 097179 - 9

Holt's English Workshop covers even more grammar and serves as a backup and support book for the Ehrenhaft text. Use this (or its successor) as a reference guide

The Rocket Review Revolution: The Ultimate Guide to the New SAT and the PSAT

Robinson, Adam. (Third (or any) Edition) New York: New American Library Trade, 2006 (and other years). Print.
This book provides excellent ideas, tips, and strategies that cover all parts of the SAT. It should be read in full detail to help improve one's SAT scores significantly. The "Rocket" Book covers strategies for each section but gives especially good advice for the verbal and essay sections.

Ten (or Eleven or Twelve) Real SATS (Practice Tests for the SAT and PSAT) - by Kaplan or Princeton Review -

Kaplan. Kaplan 12 Practice Tests for the SAT, 2012 (or any) Edition. Revised New York: Kaplan Education, 2012. Print.
Princeton Review. 11 Practice Tests for the SAT & PSAT, 2012 (or any) Edition (College Test Preparation). New York: Princeton Review. Print.

"The Real ACT Prep Guide" by Petersons (Any Edition: 2012 the latest).

Ten ACT's: Mc Graw Hill (Latest Edition)

These books do provide detailed answer explanations so that they can be used during or after your use of the "Big Blue/Online Course" combination (or for ACT Prep).

Remember that all of the books mentioned are packed with detailed advice. Read as much of the advice as possible.

In the days leading up to the exam, there are several important strategies that will help boost your score. Get a good night's sleep the evening before, and eat a healthy breakfast the morning of the exam. Arrive early to the exam room and be prepared with number 2 pencils, a calculator, water bottle, snacks for the breaks, and anything else you may need. Relax and try not to worry. You have been preparing for the exam for quite some time and you will reach your potential.

After taking the PSAT or SAT, take a deep breath. Be sure to sign up for as much feedback as is available, so that when you get your scores sent in the mail (or online) you will also get the full analysis of your mistakes; that way if you choose to take the exam again, you will know what you still need to work on. Regarding this, with many SAT/ACT exams one can order any number of analytical reports. The availability depends on which particular exam is in question (contact the SAT or ACT people for availability of this service) - May, April, June, etc. For your analytical work, order as much data as is available - and study the results to help you prep for the next time - when and if necessary. You may see patterns of mistakes on certain topics or passages you found difficult, or you may notice that you scored lower in your later sections, perhaps because of fatigue or lack of concentration. The SAT/

ACT experience is a learning process and each time you take the exam you will learn more about how you can improve.

So although the SAT/ACT process may not exactly be "fun," it can be fulfilling and rewarding especially as you note your improvement. Not only will you have new opportunities open to you due to your improvement on the SAT/ACT in terms of college admissions, but you will also feel quite accomplished with the work you have done. Succeeding on the SAT/ACT comes from within. Hopefully, with this book helping to guide you, you will soon be cruising down the path to success.

Chapter Five

A Pupil Reflects

I wanted in this chapter (and in Chapters later in the book) to give you a view of the SAT/ACT from a pupil's perspective - some who have just taken it and are heading for college and some who are about to begin the whole process. This first piece was written by a very successful pupil, Jill, who did very well in high school and is now headed to a fine college. She's a wonderful writer, as you'll see. Here is her brief SAT story. She did not take the ACT. When it's done I shall comment on it (and, as we said, more pupil musings are found later in the book).

As a junior in high school, I put off the SAT process as much as I could. I despise standardized testing, the idea of the SAT, and the long - winded route associated with preparation for it. I did not want to admit that the college process had begun and that I needed to start preparing. Needless to say, this was a terrible idea. My procrastination led me through one unsuccessful SAT class, one slightly more successful SAT tutor, two SAT exams, and a fateful hitchhiking adventure. In the end, I was satisfied with my score, got into college, and continued living a meaningful life. But the process itself? It killed me.

While I'm sure many have SAT horror stories, I have definitely lived through them all. Forgot to do your SAT homework? Been there. Soaked your College Board Handbook in the bath? Done that. Got a flat tire on the way to the SATs and needed to hitchhike to the school? Yes, I've done that too. Although I am far from knowledgeable on how to get a 2400 with ease, through my experiences I have learned a few tricks.

As a fore note, although I may be the only one who feels this way, I firmly believe that while SATs may be an integral part of the college process, they are less important than people make them out to be. There is no need to worry as if your life were to come to an end if you don't do well. This will only make you feel uncomfortable and lack assurance during the test. Rather, be confident in your abilities as a reader, analyzer, and test taker. You will do well and even if you don't, you can always retake the exam. There is no benefit to being anxious, so try to stay calm. One of my close friends once said, "People always tell us about how important the SATs are: how much they matter, how much they affect our future, how much of our poor little lives depends on these silly tests. I'm not ready, nor is anyone, but I guess we all have to go through it."

That being said, it's much more exciting to do well than mediocre and not that difficult if you are willing to put in the time. The best advice I received prior to taking the SAT was from a good friend of mine who took them a year before I did. She explained, "Take a lot of practice exams and just do a little bit each day. As long as you practice, you'll be fine." Her words ring very true. The SAT is formulaic. There are a few different types of problems that question a variety of skills that you already know. If you can practice all these different types and master the keys to answering the questions, acing the SAT should come easily. Unfortunately for us high schoolers, practicing SAT problems can be extremely tedious and boring, but it is still the best method of preparation.

If you find it difficult to schedule prep time yourself, as I did, I would highly encourage your taking a Princeton Review or Kaplan course, or getting an SAT tutor. Just remember that you still have to put in a decent amount of work on your own time if you want to be successful. When I took an SAT course at the beginning of my junior year, I did not take it half as seriously as I should have. Although I did well on the practice tests and did most of my homework, I thought that just taking the class would be sufficient to doing well. This isn't true. Later in the year, I got an SAT tutor for a period of time because I felt unprepared. This was much more suitable for me personally as the tutor could focus on my exact needs and help me schedule time for practice problems. Still, no matter what option you choose, tutor, course, or self - prep, you're going to need to do a lot of work on your own time. If you would like to mix tutoring and self-prep, I have a friend who took an online course. He really enjoyed it, and you may find that to fit your needs as well. All of these options will help guide you through a successful

SAT training procedure; you just need to choose the one best suited to your studying style.

After preparing for the exam for months, the "doomsday" will finally come. On the day of the SAT, relax. Remember that you've been taking practice exams for months, and probably have more experience than many of the other people in the room, let alone the nation. Wear comfortable clothing, bring extra batteries for your calculator, tons of pencils, water, snacks for the breaks, and personally, I like to have a pack of gum to keep my brain fully active. Don't be nervous - as I said before, the test gets more hype than it deserves, and the more confident you are, the more likely you are to succeed.

As exhausting as the SAT journey may be, I exaggerated just a bit - it won't kill you. The results will be proportional to the amount of effort you put in, so be wary. While there may be times when you want to go out for dinner with friends instead of preparing, stick to your planned practice sessions. I have definitely ditched my SAT books and even stood them up on many occasions. I've cheated on them for my preferred companions and left them alone with my number two pencils. I regret those cancelled dates as I probably could have done better if I had not procrastinated as much. Nonetheless, your SAT scores are only one part of the long college process. Success on the SATs will keep your options open in the long run. Strive to do well, but don't worry, it's just the SATs.

Jill talks about procrastination. This is common to many juniors. Perhaps they just want to put the "growing up" on hold for a while.

Her description of the hitchhiking and near - disaster on the way to the test center also gives great advice. As many teenagers are not proficient at "preparing and planning," the SAT/ACT presents them with another wonderful opportunity to sharpen these essential qualities. Getting there on time, rush free, and relaxed, is no easy chore! But it is so very important!

Jill's suggestion of the need to possess a calm attitude is quite significant. As she says, it won't really help to worry. She also discusses all that necessary practice. But especially note her "mastering the keys to answering the questions." This goes with our earlier discussion of the great need to analyze test answers to help figure out why and how correct answers are discovered. Perhaps "acing" the test might be better replaced by "realizing your potential" on the test.

Jill did point out the need for a structured approach to preparing for the SAT. Of course, as mentioned, we agree. And we believe that the one on one coaching nearly always brings out one's best. Jill also gave a great hint about test day prep - perhaps even packing an "exam prep day rescue/survival bag" replete with pencils, gum, snack, calculator, etc - everything you might need to be successful on exam day - and pack it the night (or 2) before the "super" day!

Jill was a well above average pupil so keep this in mind when you look back at this composition. Remember that pupil's thoughts and insights differ from pupil to pupil and also differ based on pupil ability level.

Chapter Six

Reading Critically

In the next section of our book, we will address the actual subject matter - the "Meat and Potatoes" of our exams. One by one, we will discuss the preliminary "ins and outs" of each phase of our exams.

Once again, we talk at first about the SAT. Although ACT Reading is somewhat different, the SAT prep that follows is similar enough. More about specific ACT Reading later.

The Critical Reading (Verbal) section of the SAT can be stressful. Twenty - five minutes to answer sentence completion and reading comprehension questions can be daunting to some. However, there is no need for it to be this way. The vocabulary section of the SAT is much less demanding than in the past: fewer words are tested and the sentence completion questions tend to be easier than the analogies, which are no longer on the SAT. Moreover, with the right techniques and practiced methods, reading comprehension passages can become less problematic.

Mastering the sentence completion sections of the SAT can thus be a quick way to boost your score. The questions are short and relatively simple as long as you understand the words. The key to success in this section is boosting your vocabulary. There are endless methods to enrich vocabulary; however, some prove to be more successful than others. Word boxes and vocabulary lists can be helpful, especially if you tend to be a visual learner. You may find it easier to remember words via other devices: reading SAT vocabulary novels is just one example. This technique will help you remember words by attaching meaning (through a story) to complex vocabulary. Others prefer to create vocabulary word index cards, with the word on one side, and the meaning on the other. These are easy to carry around and you can practice your vocabulary at any time.

Another method is to create vocabulary lists on your computer or by hand. In a chart format, you have a word, the meaning of the word, and a sentence using the word. You may even want to include a picture to help you remember the word, meaning, and sentence. For example, using the word "gregarious," you would have: Gregarious, fond of the company of others; sociable. "My gregarious friend Gregory is the life of the party; he is always happiest when he is dancing, making people laugh, and having a great time." Then, if you wanted to, you could include a picture of Greg talking with other people. Try to use real - life instances, outrageous examples, and the names of your friends to help you remember the situation and, in turn, the new vocabulary word when writing sentences. Often, the more hilarious the sentence the more likely you are to remember the word.

Thus, enriching your vocabulary can be somewhat easy. Start learning words as early as freshman or sophomore year and by the time you take the SAT you will have a much broader vocabulary. Even if you don't start learning sophisticated words until your junior year, practice and reinforcement is what it takes to improve your vocabulary skills and your critical reading score. Using a list, (or word box) such as "Hot 1000 SAT Words" (or any other vocabulary word list for the SAT found online, in a Princeton Review, Kaplan, College Board, or other SAT book), choose, say five words a night and learn them via your method of choice. Practice the words until you know them well, and then try to use the words the next day in everyday conversation, if you can. Such reinforcement will help you remember the words. Unfortunately, many people find SAT vocabulary learning to be tedious and silly, with no immediate rewards. Learning words to boost your score will take time, but laziness will never help you. By spending at least 5 to 10 minutes a night learning a few new words, after a while, your score will increase because you will consistently answer more of the sentence completion questions correctly.

Again, I find that often pupils get quite lazy, especially on vocabulary prep. They just don't seem to consistently study their words as they need to. They find every excuse for this tough process. As we said, the process can be broken down into simpler "bite size" pieces - e.g.- learn 4 words per night - or 3 - or 5 - or whatever the pupil can handle. After long periods of time, hundreds of words can be learned and the probability of a higher SAT verbal score increases dramatically.

In addition, both long term and short term, via increasing vocabulary, the pupil can very nicely increase his speaking, writing and reading abilities. Some pupils prefer to use, and have fun with, mnemonic picture vocabulary books that make learning the words go much quicker for many. Earlier we made mention of The Rocket Review Revolution: The Ultimate Guide to the New SAT. This book, as discussed, gives some great suggestions for enhancing SAT performance in nearly all areas. Here we see that his sections on vocabulary/reading comprehension are no exception - his points are helpful in enhancing performance in these areas as well. Refer to it!

In addition to mastering the actual vocabulary on the SAT, there are a few other tricks helpful for success in this part of the "verbal" section. Let's discuss one: Before looking at the answer options for the sentence completion questions, write down your own words that would work in the blanks. This way you avoid being tricked by more difficult questions and can quickly answer correctly. If you aren't certain of what type of words fit in the blanks, you can usually tell, at the very least, for those specific two blank spaces whether the two words are similar or opposite. Also, look for key words to give you an idea about how the two blanks are linked - these key words might be "but," "and," "or," "not," to name just a few. For example:

> Hoping to_____ the argument between the disrupting pupils, the principal suggested a compromise that he felt would be _____ to both students.
>
>   (A) enforce . . . helpful
>   (B) halt . . . divisive
>   (C) overcome . . . unappealing
>   (D) continue . . . pleasing
>   (E) settle . . . acceptable

If you can think of your own words to put in, such as, alleviate (for blank one) and agreeable (for blank two), this will help you find the right answer choice by matching your words with similar words. If you couldn't think of your own words, you know that the first and second blank have to be in concord with each other because of the phrasing of the sentence and the key word "compromise." The correct answer is (E) settle . . . acceptable, and as you can see, it was similar to alleviate . . . agreeable, whereas no other options were even remotely comparable. By using these skills and studying vocabulary, you will have more time for the reading comprehension passages as you will be moving through the first several questions of the critical reading section with less of a struggle. Keep in mind however, there is truly no substitute for knowing the word and that can only be accomplished by reading and carefully studying word lists.

Many people who are skilled readers and writers have trouble with the critical reading section of the SAT or ACT, but don't let this discourage you (we will provide you with strategies to help you maximize your potential). The passages can be fiction or non - fiction, long or short, single or paired, with topics ranging from humanities, to social studies, natural sciences, and literary fiction. The passages also vary in style and can include narrative, argumentative, and expository elements. Some are difficult, whereas others are simpler to read and understand. Despite the variety of passage options, the critical reading section can be somewhat formulaic and the reading comprehension questions are all more or less similar. There are three major broad categories of questions: vocabulary in context, literal comprehension, and extended reasoning. While this may sound complicated, after taking practice tests and working on skills (the oft - mentioned analysis by detailed examination of answers), answering questions to these passages should come more easily.

There are numerous techniques, strategies, and methods for approaching the questions in the reading comprehension sections. Since time management is a factor, depending on how fast and quickly you can answer the questions, you may want to choose a more time efficient strategy. When practicing, try out different methods, and see what is best for you. Once you find a method that seems to consistently work, stick to that process and follow it rigorously during prep and on test day. Remember, not all strategies will be best for you, so it essential that you find <u>your</u> most successful method, and the only way you can do that is through practice. In formulating your "attack" strategy for reading comprehension questions, try out, as we've said, different methods. Although most strategy books (and me) suggest a method of partially "skimming" passages, reading the questions and then answering them, others suggest, e.g., reading the questions before reading the passage. Try all methods. Find what's best for you and stick with it. Your practice will help you to pinpoint your best method. We will continue to discuss the various methods. Once again, we will discuss whatever differences exist between SAT and ACT reading prep soon.

Although different test prep companies (for ACT/SAT) will advocate creative techniques, there are some practices that reliably provide results. For long (SAT) passages, read closely the beginning and end of the passage and skim the middle. You would then jot down notes along the sides of the passage and underline anything you think is an essential part of the essay. Then, when you read the questions (after the story), you cover the answer choices (reading just the question "stem" - i.e., the actual question), and try to formulate an answer without looking at the choices. This process will help you avoid getting tricked by the "fake-outs" that the SAT or ACT has as answer choices. On the SAT, where there might be some shorter passages, you should still read the passage first but since they might be so short, skimming may not be quite enough. We are always trying not only to be time efficient but also to help you get the most answers correct.

You will also come across (on SAT) paired passages, which can often be frustrating. Paired passages are related essays on a shared issue or theme that you are asked to compare and contrast. For paired passages (both short and especially long), read the first passage first, answer the questions that apply to the first passage, read the second passage next, answer the questions that apply to the second passage, and finally answer the questions that apply to comparing both passages. For these paired passages, follow the same analytical process as you did on the long single passages - read/skim the passage and then answer the questions first by formulating your own response. Although this may sound confusing, as you do your practice passages it will become clearer.

As general advice, if you can eliminate any of the answer choices (even one, and you will usually be able to eliminate more than one), and thus narrow down your possibilities, it is wise to go ahead and answer the question (or, in this case, "guess"). Sometimes, it is difficult to be completely sure of your answer because of the confusing phrasing on the SAT/ACT, but if you use the process of elimination, especially by finding support for your chosen answers from the passage, you will be right more often than not.

No matter what techniques you use, in order to be successful on this part of the SAT/ACT, the key is again practice and close examination of your choice patterns. Be sure to <u>analyze</u> every practice test you take! If, e.g., you are doing practice questions from College Board's "The Official SAT Study Guide" (Big Blue), you can sign up (as we've discussed) to discover the detailed answer explanations online at collegeboard.com. If you are doing your practice questions out of the Princeton Review or Kaplan books, the answers will be located in the back of the given section you're working on. Strategies, in this case, depend on your choice of practice material!

Don't simply look at the answer and mark it as right or wrong, but be sure to <u>read and analyze the explanation</u> (we repeat this over and over) as to why the correct answer is the one that it is. If you were stuck between two answer choices, make sure you understand why the right answer choice is C, e.g., and not D. You must find reasons why wrong answer choices are indeed incorrect.

Try to practice regular sleep patterns (to increase concentration) both the night before the test as well as during your latter prep period. Concentration is essential to successful SAT/ACT reading skill and will also aid in every other aspect of the SAT/ACT. Studies have found that students often lose focus as the test progresses, and often critical reading scores seem to reflect this in that they fall in the latter parts of the test. In order to maintain a steady and consistent score, you need to be able to pace yourself, concentrate and be mentally and physically in shape.

Chapter Seven

Mathematically Speaking

The math section of the SAT (ACT math discussion will take place shortly). This section can be quite challenging. Scores absolutely can improve but they don't seem to increase quite as easily as they do on the writing/grammar section. However, when the "right" procedures are implemented, scores do rise, often dramatically.

Again, as with all parts of the SAT, it is quite helpful to get a "baseline" score for oneself. In other words, one should get that "initial" reading on one's starting point, that is, just where they "are at" mathematically. How does one accomplish this? Let's review: by any number of ways. Tenth graders should absolutely take the PSAT, when it is given, in the fall of that sophomore year. (Some schools, for various reasons, do not allow some tenth graders to take the PSAT. For example, the school might believe that more math is necessary for the pupil to be "PSAT - ready," which they will be in a year). The results may be quite accurate as far as predictability of SAT status at that point. For example, a tenth grader gets a 50 (500) on the PSAT math section. This score is pretty accurate, I find, as far as serving as a good starting point of math pupil ability at that moment in time. With study and practice, scores will absolutely rise. The 11th grade PSAT serves a similar purpose. However, since its offering is so close to the actual SAT (winter or spring of grade 11), it is even more effective as a prediction and guidance tool.

Other helpful diagnostic exams, as we've said, are the Kaplan and Princeton Review full - length SAT practice tests. To reiterate, these companies offer pupils proctored practice on full length SAT exams (which are even better than the abridged PSAT's). Pupils register with the given company and sign up to take these exams, which are then presented under realistic conditions. Results of these exams provide feedback of a rather extensive and analytical nature - perfect for diagnosing pupil needs. Test results serve to classify students into various baseline (before practice) ability levels, and pupils themselves, tutors and/or other "coaches" can address individual needs. Again, one may use one of the exam prep books to take a practice test on one's own.

Now to some specifics of math SAT improvement. I have been tutoring pupils for the SAT/ACT for many years and have worked with hundreds of pupils. I consider myself a great expert on what it takes to improve your SAT/ACT scores. One size does not fit all but there are some "common" ideas and practices of which all pupils should be aware. When implemented, these common practices will be of help to all!

"Know" the SAT (ACT discussion later) math section, its structure and composition. On the first page of the math sections are some common formulas. All should be familiar with these formulas. Pupils should start working SAT problems beginning with problem #1 (usually the most basic question) up through the end of the given math section. As the pupils will notice, the problems increase in difficulty on the math section. It is essential that pupils get (as many as possible of) the "easies" and "mediums" correct. The "hards" can be quite difficult, but if many of only the "easies" and "mediums" are correct, excellent scores can be achieved.

In working on number one and beyond, each time a pupil gets one wrong, the analysis must begin. Why was it done incorrectly? Was it wrong because of carelessness? Or, was it that the pupil just did not know the math needed to get it right?

To enhance scores, this analysis is critical on all sections. Without these insightful analyses, math scores will not "move" much.

Each time one discovers that there is a math deficit (lack of math knowledge, be it formula - related or math mechanics), it is crucial that the pupil learn the material and strategy needed to solve that particular problem. It would also help greatly if the pupil were to write down this strategy (or bit of math knowledge) on a list that is tailor - made for the particular pupil at hand; for example, "Mike's Math List." The next time that this type of math problem were to arise, the pupil would likely get it right and, in general, with each correct answer, scores rise by about ten points.

Pupils studying completely on their own should use this method of recording "new topics I've learned" or "questions that I still have." Then, if they still need help in understanding, they can always network with friends, teachers, and the internet.

Related to this, a brief aside (again) on your prep choice. As discussed previously, when you decide to truly get down to test prep, you will need to choose whether to get a private tutor, sign up for a course or go it fully on your own (with or without help from friends, internet, or other resources). Decisions here are based on personal preference, financial considerations, learning style, etc. One of the major purposes of this book is to help guide you, advise you, and support you through the entire SAT/ACT prep process no matter which method of preparation you choose. Sometimes in my discussions I may relate what I would do in the "one - on - one" tutoring situation. The advice I give can usually be used equally well either by the pupil who is preparing totally on his own or by the pupil who signs up for a course. Remember, tailor your prep to what's best for you. Some pupils experiment and try more than one method.

If you decide to go with tutoring, the "analysis" we referred to earlier is why, in general, one - on - one tutoring is more effective than large or even small group instruction. In one - on - one, question analysis and math knowledge can be tailored to that one particular pupil - the given student doesn't have to sit through many questions (and in addition lose lots of time) in reviewing topics that others in the group don't understand but that our student in question does know well.

Now it is true that on the math SAT, many of the questions can be solved with very basic math knowledge. However, as we've seen, questions sequentially build in degree of difficulty, they get "trickier" and more "riddle - like" in nature. I often use a riddle book to demonstrate the "tricky" nature of many math problems. This is key. The only way you get better at solving these types of problems is by doing them, analyzing them, and then doing more of them . . . and then more and more . . . and repeating this procedure over and over, day after day. The more you do, the better . . . and better . . . you get!

To some extent pupils can perform these procedures on their own. As with reading comprehension, you do require a good answer guide that provides not only answers but detailed explanations - not only of correct choices, but ideally, also explanations of why wrong answers are indeed wrong. Many of the suggested books possess this quality. As with the verbal section, the best book is the large blue book put out by the College Board - "Big Blue," with its companion piece - the College Board "Online Course." Big Blue is the great practice book it is mainly because it is published by the College Board - the very people who create the SAT. Thus, the questions are more accurate and realistic than any other prep book. As with the verbal section, the problem is that "Big Blue" lacks answer explanations - containing only correct answer letters. Useless for the all important analysis that needs to be performed. That is why the "Online Course" should be purchased! We discussed the details of this issue earlier in the book. For pupils prepping on their own (as well as all others), the course is extremely helpful.

As with verbal, there are more practice materials for math. There are books like those previously mentioned (published by Kaplan, Princeton Review and Mc Graw Hill). These books are good. They are updated yearly and are very similar to "Big Blue," the big difference being that they do contain answers with those critical explanations. In addition, you don't need to go online to work with these books - the books are thus user friendly and quite portable. They don't, however, go into the same detail as the SAT College Board's "Online Course." They are effective however.

For math help, there are other books as well, probably the best of which are: "The Rocket Review Revolution: The Ultimate Guide to the New SAT" by Adam Robinson (previously mentioned); and "The New SAT - Insider's Guide" by Fiske and Hammond (ISBN #: 1 - 4002 - 0163 - X: this or later edition). Strategies for attacking the math section, as well as all the other areas of the SAT, are given. And these strategies can be quite helpful. Again, important reading for all test "preppers."

This leads us to another review thought regarding the math section. Pupils may often require the expert assistance of a math teacher or other math expert when analyzing math problems. There will be several problems that are difficult for many (depending on pupil ability) to comprehend, even after reading the detailed explanations that are offered by the various publications. Here is where tutor or teacher expertise is often required in order for the study methodology to be truly effective. Thus, for many of you who decide to prep totally on your own, there will usually come a point, as mentioned, when you simply cannot solve a problem, even after using your book resources, without outside intervention. Here is where you need to call on a friend or relative, ask your teacher, or go to the internet and try to post your question to a math help website.

Thus, the solving of these math "riddles" must be done slowly and methodically. The pupil needs lots of analytical practice. This method over time will usually result in enhanced grades. I tell the story of one girl I had tutored. She received a 47 (470) in math on her grade eleven PSAT. However, she had been in accelerated math classes in school. Why so low (for a pupil like her) on the PSAT? She just wasn't used to the trickiness and ambiguous nature of many of the questions on the SAT (again, we discuss ACT math later). Little by little she began doing math problems. She used the practice tests to engage herself in "tons" of exercises. She actually started to enjoy her math work. Soon, her proficiency began to improve - rather rapidly. Her enormous devotion to practice and analysis led her to a March Math SAT score of 730 - a 260 point increase! (What % increase is this? Well, 260 / 470 = 55 %). That, by the way, illustrates the methodology of calculating % increase - a definite topic on the SAT and ACT! This dramatic score enhancement is possible for all, but only with hard work, effective analysis, and dedication.

Another youngster I worked with, as previously mentioned, had a similar (although not quite as great) rise in his math score. For him, practice also became "fun." When he had some free time, he chose to spend it with Big Blue, the online College Board course, and the Princeton Review text. It became relaxing for him as he truly enjoyed the prep work. Engaging in math practice gave him the same great feeling he received when he played basketball.

Usually, this level of "nirvana" is not attained by most; however, if one can "push" oneself to practice practice practice, near miraculous results can be achieved.

Let's discuss some more important points for math section success. Pupils of all math ability levels often get sloppy and careless. One must concentrate! Often pupils get lazy - they try to do the math "in their heads" - without using the scrap areas provided and even at times without using their calculators.

Another point - use a graphing calculator - like the TI-83 e.g. Many pupils are knowledgeable about graphing calculator use - but many still are not. Learn its use well! Working "in your head" often leads to careless errors and loss of valuable points - often on the "must get right" easy and medium level questions! We say "must get it right," because, as mentioned earlier, pupils can receive superb SAT scores in math simply by getting the majority of the "easy and medium" (levels 1-4) questions right. The College Board publications usually rank questions (from 1 - 5) by degree of difficulty. Many pupils worry about getting the really challenging questions right. Don't! Even many teachers have trouble with these level five questions. Get as many of the easy and medium questions right as is possible. Spend most of your time on them. Even pupils who consider themselves quite "weak" in math will surprise themselves with decent scores if they take one question at a time, use their pens and pencils to do scrap work, focus time and energy on the easier and medium questions and analyze and learn from their mistakes.

Of course pupils need to be careful to shade in the correct circles and not err in this area. Pupils must be aware of the mechanical procedures for math "grid - in" questions and of the philosophy of and penalties for "guessing." Again, on the SAT there is a small penalty for wrong answers (thus "guessing" must be considered carefully); on the ACT there is no penalty for incorrect responses, so one should "guess away!!" As we've said, for the (SAT) verbal section, if one can eliminate just one choice, guessing might be indicated. Knowledge about guessing includes knowing that SAT math grid - in questions, e.g., carry no penalty for incorrect answers, yet all other math questions do elicit minor penalties for wrong answers.

Time is always a factor and pupils need to practice test - taking under timed conditions. In addition, anyone entitled to extra time must be sure to file for it!

Again, use your pen or pencil and scrap areas to avoid those frequent errors that can be made by juggling the numbers in your head.

Often pupils get lazy in other ways too. They don't practice as much as they should and they just look up answers without analyzing the examples. What happens then is disastrous - they keep making the same mistakes over and over - and never improve. As mentioned, I've seen SAT math scores go from 470 to 730. Yes! Over time, with practice, proper strategies and motivation, these and similar types of improvements can and do occur.

Stay in touch with Collegeboard.com (and ACTstudent.org) to keep current on the latest practice problems, strategies and insights. Collegeboard. com has much to offer. There is the "question of the day" and there are offers for many wonderful publications that can help you (the student and/or his parent) navigate not only SAT prep but also the choppy waters of the college application process. In addition, you can learn about scholarship opportunities and financial aid. ACTStudent.org is quite useful as well.

Also, keep in mind that as you take more and more math through grade ten and eleven, your math ability is naturally, in most cases, going to improve.

Of course we have in math (as in all other areas) pupils of varying ability levels. We have the math "superstars," i.e., those who could achieve near 800 before the studying even gets under way. And we have those who struggle to break 300; i.e., those who've been having math difficulty likely since they began first grade. And, we have those in the middle. The prep for these varied groups is, as we've seen, different.

The 750-800 pupil must be greatly challenged - peppered with many level 5 (hardest) type problems. This advanced pupil must deal mainly with the really tough "riddle" type problems, yet continue to guard against overconfidence and carelessness. When prepping on your own, (or with help) keep this in mind. There are some books out there that will help in preparing the "Einstein" type math pupil. They are books that provide extremely challenging math problems. The math problems found in them are highly challenging. Search for them on the Internet.

As for the 300 - 400 (and below) level pupils, their math skills usually need major enhancement. They need that remediation so that they will have better odds of doing well and eventually will be challenged by those level five questions. They too can absolutely dramatically improve their math skills, their self - confidence, and their odds of getting into the college of their dreams. How does this latter student, the one who has always been heavily challenged by math, improve? In any number of ways.

It's usually quite difficult at this lower level to repair his math deficits on his own. He really needs to have someone guide and assist him. It can be a friend, a relative, a tutor, a teacher. This helper will guide him through the remedial work that will be necessary to raise his math ability to the next level. As he learns new topics and reviews old ones he will need to practice these newly acquired skills. This practice must be done diligently and can be done on his own. This process of remediation and targeted analytical practice will help him become a much more proficient math student. As he improves, his self - esteem will increase and there'll be no stopping him or his climb to math success!

So we see that often there is the need for a trained one on one tutor or coach, who is able to diagnose ability, calculate need and move in with math enhancement strategies tailored to fit the needs of the unique student at hand.

Thus, this completes, for now, the (ongoing) summary by this 38 year teaching veteran (me) on how to improve math SAT scores.

Chapter Eight

Do The Write Thing (The Essay)

As we've discussed, the SAT essay comprises 30% of the "Writing" section, with the balance emanating from the "rules of grammar" (multiple choice questions). So how to do well on this essay? By the way, the ACT essay is quite similar. However, once again, we will discuss this essay in more detail in later chapters.

It is a good idea to read up on the ABC's of the SAT (and ACT) essay. There are several places to go in order for you to gain more essay expertise. First, is the already mentioned "Ultimate Guide to the New SAT" by Robinson. It is great for essay help. Then there is "Insider's Guide to the New SAT" by Fiske (also mentioned). Reading the essay chapters in these and in your other prep guides (e.g., Kaplan, Princeton Review, Big Blue, Barron's) you will be helped to become a very successful SAT essay writer. You should also consult with an English teacher or a tutor for feedback and suggestions on your essay writing process. Often you can locate SAT essay experts online who can give you feedback (perform a search). The creative writing you do in your regular English classes with its teacher feedback can help the most.

Since it is basically a 25 - 30 minute speed writing assignment, certain considerations become significant. One should spend the first few minutes making an outline. Then, in most cases, the 5 paragraph essay formula is recommended - introduction, conclusion with 3 support paragraphs in the middle. The 5 paragraph formula is only a suggestion. There truly is no exact formula or style that will earn superior essay grades. Good writing and organization will, of course, rate highly. Many sample essays can be located in the appropriate sections of Big Blue and Big Red.

Essay scores can range from 0 to 12 (combined from both raters). Some excellent writers often wind up with a very average score of 6 or 7. This occurs mainly because pupils who first begin learning about the essay do not have a handle on SAT essay - writing techniques. Perhaps they don't truly answer the question, they don't provide enough support for their thesis, their essays are disorganized, they run out of time, and/or they did not outline adequately.

All of these problems are often solved by following the procedures already delineated. That is, consult with the prep guides, learn how to create a good essay, get lots of practice in school, and network with people who can provide you with feedback on your writings. In our book we do not give you the actual logistics of essay writing . . . however, we have referred you to specific books that do.

If you know your writing ability is poor at this stage, you may need to get lots of help now, and then again down the road. If you need this major work on grammar, spelling, organizing, outlining, etc, then it must be done! Hopefully, in your school, you're receiving extra writing support. Perhaps you can get help as well from tutors, family members or even friends who can help guide you to better writing skills. You can always maximize and improve on your current abilities.

As we have said, pupils need to prepare for the essay on the "New" SAT (March 2005 was the first sitting of this "New" Exam). Pupils must adequately answer the assigned essay question. They must organize their response (this is where outlining helps). They must refer to experiences, observations, literature, and/or history. Their examples must be specific, appropriate, and adequate. Pupils must practice their essay writing under time pressure.

Here is a critical part of essay - writing preparation: The practice essay is written. It must then receive a thorough analysis. Did it satisfy SAT requirements? How well in general was it written? This is where the aforementioned feedback by an expert comes into play.

An expert teacher or proficient writer must analyze your practice essay. Preferably, the analyst is an English teacher or writing specialist trained in the SAT/ACT grading rubrics, or a friend or relative who can also offer excellent feedback. As far as the "rubrics," these are delineated, e.g., in Big Blue and in Big Red. The "rubrics" should be studied by all. They provide guidelines or characteristics of an essay which would earn a 6 (maximum by one rater), or a 5, etc. Our prepping pupils must learn all that they can about the nature of the essay and how to achieve success with it.

Very often pupils simply have little or no idea of how to compose this essay in order to receive a maximum grade. This teacher feedback provides invaluable assistance in this area. There is another way to get feedback on your essay. Many of the books you will use (e.g. Petersons, Princeton Review, and "Big Blue") may (at least at one time did) provide a service whereby they instantly grade your essay using computer technology. In other words, you E-mail your essay to them and within seconds they grade it. It is usually done by some form of "automatic" scoring. It provides some help but truly a "live" grader is highly preferable. You could also "google" SAT/ACT essay grading support and see if your search yields any results.

As we mentioned, there is also that critical extra preparatory reading that the pupil should do. In Big Blue, e.g., there are a large number of pages that cover essay writing strategies. In addition there are at least two model essays (including 12 responses) that have been thoroughly analyzed in Big Blue. Multiple responses with grading rationales are given with these essays.

In the aforementioned College Board.com "online course," many sample essays are analyzed in major detail. Pupils need to learn outlining and the tailoring of their essays to satisfy the SAT graders.

As with the multiple choice part of the grammar section, pupils often go into the SAT "cold" as far as the essay. One does need to prep for it, get to know its requirements and practice it.

Chapter Nine

Is It "Sally and Me," or "Sally and I?"
The Grammar Section

What about the "new" (new since 2005) grammar section? As we mentioned, the grammar piece is 70% of the "Writing" section of the SAT (the rest is the essay). It consists of multiple choice questions essentially based on ten major areas of grammar. These areas are roughly; subject - verb agreement, pronoun usage, English idiom, parallel structure, diction, adjective/adverb use, verb choice, verb tense, modifiers (dangling, misplaced) and use of commas and other punctuation marks. There are no questions on spelling.

Grammar, as indicated, has been on the SAT since 2005. I have found that most high schools in my area do not seem to teach much pure grammar at all. In fact many of my pupils, at the beginning of our work together, can't define a verb, don't have any idea of what a preposition is and know very little about any other (major) grammar as well.

Thus when pupils take the PSAT as tenth graders (which, as mentioned I urge them to do), their grammar scores are often quite low. That is, we can have really good language arts students coming in with PSAT grammar scores consistently in the 400s (or lower). Of course there are exceptions. Some pupils have been fortunate enough to have had (often in middle school or private school) teachers along the way who did teach grammar extensively.

To encourage schools to more thoroughly teach formal grammar, this section was added to the SAT in 2005. However, grammar instruction still has not been effected at many schools.

Pupils who struggle with their language arts classes in school usually also end up with low grammar/writing scores. However, their SAT and ACT grammar scores can dramatically increase as the students learn, study, and practice the rules of grammar. Again, as we have discussed earlier, our book of (first) choice for all pupils is Barron's SAT II Writing Fourth Edition ISBN #: 13: 978 - 0 - 7641 - 2346 - 7 by George Ehrenhaft (in the future we refer to it as "Barrons"). Pupils preparing on their own or even with a tutor should use this book (or later editions if this one is no longer available). Order from BarnesandNoble.com or Amazon.com. Old copies should still be quite available!!

When pupils learn about and practice with all of the necessary grammar rules, scores can often balloon rather quickly and consistently.

How does one prepare for this grammar piece - either on one's own or with a tutor? As mentioned, I have found that the test prep book by "Barrons" is amazing. It is well organized, well written, and extremely effective in teaching all of the required topics on the grammar test.

When tutoring, I assign readings and exercises to pupils from the Barrons book. This however is not quite sufficient. For all but the most diligent and gifted pupils, multiple readings of and note taking based on the Barrons Book (using their study skills) are often required. Thus I usually wind up reviewing the chapters with my pupils as well as providing them with review notes based on the chapters. Of course, pupils can choose to prep totally on their own! Barrons is always the place to begin!

If you're preparing with a Kaplan or Princeton Review type course, these companies will have their own grammar test prep materials. However, "Barrons" is great for self prep. As just described, read the appropriate material, do the exercises, take notes on your readings and then use your SAT exam books (like "Big Blue") for practice on real SAT/ACT - type grammar questions. As usual, always analyze your responses.

"Barron's," incidentally, had been used to prep for the SAT II in Writing, which was discontinued in March 2005 with the advent of the "New SAT I" (which now incorporates the old SAT II Writing topics). Thus, that Barron's manual was and is tailor made for your grammar and essay - writing prep. Again, those old manuals (4th Edition) are still available. Barrons did replace the 4th edition with newer, similar manuals - same idea just not quite as wonderful. So in your prep work, try to secure that 4th edition (Amazon.com, BarnesandNoble.com, etc.).

Colleges still seem to put most emphasis on the critical reading and math sections but excellent writing scores will certainly not hurt and colleges are able to view the actual student essay on line.

In addition, as another benefit of their enhanced grammar skills, pupils will be able to speak more effectively, write more effectively, and with their verbal prep included, students will acquire a much broader vocabulary. They will carry these skills throughout their lives. They will even get to turn the tables on their parents and correct their parents' errors in grammar - and be right!

To supplement "Barron's," I usually suggest "English Workshop" by Holt Publications. With help from your school, it can be ordered with an answer guide so that pupils can receive even more grammar practice. Its ISBN # is 0 - 03 - 097179 -9 (get it, or similar from, e.g., Amazon.com).

As we have said, once these grammar rules are learned effectively, pupils need to practice with SAT - type questions. They should proceed directly to Big Blue first (in combination with the online course answer guide) and then to one of the other similar publications.

It is important for pupils to be aware (and they will see) that the grammar section is composed of three different parts. Take a look at any practice SAT. There are "improving sentences" (pick the best sentence of five), "identifying sentence errors in one sentence," and "improving paragraphs." These three different types of grammar questions are all based on the (ten or so) core grammar topics mentioned earlier. Instruction and practice, be it by tutors or on their own with prep books, must be tailored to deal with these varied question types.

We now have pupils applying their sharpened grammar skills directly to the SAT practice questions (Big Blue, etc). They once again need to answer each question and then meticulously and relentlessly analyze the correct answer as well as the incorrect choices. By doing this grammar analysis over and over with more and more questions, SAT grammar scores will slowly (or quickly) improve. Their understanding of the rules of grammar will become deeply ingrained in their memories.

Remember that the pupil writing score is essentially composed of 70% grammar (multiple choice) factored in with 30% essay. This discussion of preparation procedure explains how grammar scores can often shoot up for pupils in often short periods of time!

Chapter Ten

But What About the ACT??

What about this ACT? Many of the students where I teach (in New Jersey) do not take it, and don't even know much about it. But I'll tell you one thing - they should definitely take it. There's truly nothing to lose by trying this test. When the scores come back, if pupils don't do well (or they are not exactly what they want) they can simply cancel the results (by simply not sending them) and scores will be "wiped off" their record - no one will ever see them. Colleges won't receive them. This is permitted. It's "Score Choice." Nothing to lose! What can be better than that? (For the Class of 2010, and beyond, the same procedure - ability to "throw out" unwanted scores - will also be in effect for the SAT).

Regarding this "Score Choice:" Please go to both the SAT and ACT web sites to read up on all the details and "fine print" regarding this program so that you will be thoroughly familiar with its detailed rules and regulations. There are many different ingredients in the program, and many colleges differ in their procedures for each exam, including "super scoring" (more or less taking the "best" scores from all the exams one takes).

The test (ACT) is similar to the SAT in some ways and quite different in other ways. It's certainly worth looking into.

The preparation for it is quite similar to your SAT prep. There are differences though.

First, the "ACT Company," like the College Board (creators of the SAT) puts out a "Big Blue" book too. Only the ACT's is "Big Red" - it's red and big. Its introductory section, that pupils need to read, covers everything from A to Z about the ACT. Essential reading. Like the "SAT People," they also have a superb "orientation booklet" called "Preparing for the ACT," usually available from the student's high school guidance department (or online at www.ACTstudent.org).

Big Red, extremely well - done, offers (now) five real ACT exams that were previously given to pupils. As opposed to Big Blue, Big Red offers its answers with detailed explanations - excellent for your all - important practice. As mentioned, there is a web site (www.ACTstudent.org) that offers some support (although not quite as elaborate as that of the SAT). Nearly all colleges accept ACT scores and SAT results equally.

Now let's get a bit more specific about similarities and differences between the two exams. First, the critical reading section. The passages seem to be more interesting and not quite as tricky on the ACT. They favor good readers. On the SAT, great readers often do not reach their potential because some of the questions are often so difficult to evaluate. The choices on SAT can be more confusing. For problem readers, obviously, the problems are magnified.

On the other hand, it seems that the ACT requires a bit more actual comprehensive reading in that it's difficult to get away with the "skimming" that the SAT at times calls for. Since the questions are a little more confusing on the SAT (at least at higher difficulty levels), time can be a factor. Often "skimming" is a necessary strategy on the SAT. It seems that ACT passages, perhaps dealing with more interesting topics, contain questions that, although perhaps a bit less confusing, do require more comprehensive reading (and maybe less skimming - unless skimming becomes necessary due to time pressures) of the entire passage. In the end, however, the two exams are quite similar in this area in that reading is reading. Get Big Red and work on the reading passages. See what you think. The answers and explanations are all there and the analytical study process is the same as that for the SAT. When it really comes down to it, the reading on the ACT seems a "tad" easier and also a bit more interesting.

When discussing ACT reading, it is critical to address the issue of "timing."

Let's look a bit closer at this timing on the ACT. Some pupils will receive "extended time" (mostly those in special education possessing an "IEP"). However, most will have the traditional time that is standard for all ACT exams. This time factor is of critical importance for the ACT Reading. It is as if the test taker is a jockey or a runner and must always be aware of the "pace."

So what about the timing issue? As we mentioned, there are four reading selections. Since pupils have a total of 35 minutes for the section, this works out to 8 ¾ minutes per section.

The pupil really needs to stick to the pace in order to finish all questions. Here is where practice truly will pay off. The pupil needs to work on multiple selections with the usual analysis. However, he needs to practice with his eye on the clock - learning how, if necessary, to skim more effectively (or to take a course in "speed" reading). Many ACT reading questions do not refer pupils back to specific lines as often as occurs on the SAT. This provides even more of a challenge for the reader.

Vocabulary is not directly tested on the ACT, as it is on the SAT vocabulary section. On the ACT, vocabulary is examined only indirectly as incorporated in a reading passage or on the English (grammar) section.

How about math? The SAT requires that pupils have knowledge of pretty basic math - nothing even involving trigonometry. There now (in 2013) is some Algebra Two material on the SAT, but nothing too rigorous. There are usually 3 math sections on the SAT and the big challenge, as we've indicated, is that problems, even those of medium difficulty, can be extremely tricky, confusing and "riddle - like." On the SAT the pupil is given some math formulas to consult whereas the ACT does not provide this service. However, the formulas presented are mostly basic and can be memorized fairly easily.

The ACT, by the way, has only one math section, one English section, one critical reading section, one science section, and an essay. Each of the five sections of the ACT is longer than any of the ten SAT sections. So the logistics of the exams are different. ACT math is 60 minutes for 60 questions.

ACT math is fairly straightforward, and in that way, quite similar to the SAT II (the one hour long SAT "subject" test - more about it later on) and thus more an achievement test. The SAT II in Math (either of the two versions) is, however, considerably more challenging than the ACT Math. On the ACT, if you know the math basics of the problem, you'll likely get the problem right. No games, few tricks and riddles. Sounds good? It is. The only "problem" is that for the ACT you really need to know a bit more math (goes deeper into the HS curriculum) and know it more thoroughly than you need to know it for the SAT.

For example, on the ACT, you will need to know some trigonometry, questions on logarithms, the unit circle, reciprocal trig functions and a few other extra topics. Now questions on these enhanced topics tend to be quite straightforward but in your prep work for the ACT, you need to be sure that you've learned most topics in the curriculum that appear in Big Red. You can self - learn or receive tutoring in these topics before test day. In these "extra" topics, we're not talking here about a very large amount of material. If you do not master these topics it will not be a huge problem as good scores can be achieved without them. Pupils for whom math is a big problem should also try ACT math (even if they are not familiar with all necessary curriculum materials). There are, on the ACT, as we've said, more straight-forward non-trick questions. There is no penalty for wrong answers and one doesn't necessarily need mastery of large amounts of material to achieve very attractive grades. The ACT math results may be a pleasant surprise for many, especially those who've never considered this exam option previously.

To summarize: ACT math, although containing a few more topics, is less tricky by far, contains more relatively easy problems, and favors the students who know their math basics well. Thus, nothing to lose, practice with analysis, take the real test and compare your results to the SAT math.

Next is the ACT "English" section. This parallels the SAT "Writing" Section. The prep you did for the SAT in this area (with Barron's SAT II and English Workshop) will prepare you well for the ACT. There are a few additional topics that you might want to study in "English Workshop" and/ or another grammar text. These additional topics include: more extensive knowledge of punctuation, including commas, apostrophes, colons, dashes, and exclamation marks; Also, there is a bit more of sentence structure. Big Red also elaborates more on grammar details in their publication.

I have found that the English section of the ACT is somewhat easier than that of the SAT. Once again, the questions are more straightforward and less "riddle - like." Get Big Red, study the preliminary material in it, do the practice tests, and analyze your answers. For more practice on the ACT, register on their website and use the practice there and/or get the ACT prep books published by Kaplan, Mc Graw Hill, and the Princeton Review.

The essay on the ACT is quite similar to that on the SAT. However, it is even better as it is not urgent that you reference specific examples from literature and history, e.g., to illustrate your point. On the SAT, it is preferable that you do use examples from your studies (history, literature, etc). On the ACT essay you are free to use more creativity. The ACT essay is five minutes longer and the topics more general and less "cerebral."

However, there is one bigger difference between the two exams: It is the ACT science section. The SAT has no science section. Even though it is "science," you do not really have to prepare for the science section by studying science topics, formulas, or anything resembling the usual science test prep. What you are given is a series of seven sets of scientific data, each presented in various formats - graphs, charts, tables, experiments, etc. You must answer questions based on this information.

Thus, the pupil does not prepare for the science section as he would for an "in school" bio or chem test. Therefore, the student does need to know the material before taking the exam, only to comprehend and interpret the given information that is presented. However, it would be great practice if the student were to sharpen his skills of analytical technical reading - the kinds of skills also needed to help comprehend detailed social studies, math, history, and/or science material. This reading skill is yet another important one to practice since it will be quite useful in college and thereafter. If one achieves this valuable interpretative skill, one will do well on this science section. This science section should be practiced slowly, carefully and deliberately.

We conclude that the science section may indeed favor a pupil who is a good reader, as this section is truly one that requires reading comprehension, analytical thought, and concentration and focus, rather than demanding pure scientific knowledge. There is that time pressure again on ACT Science: many questions with not a great amount of time.

An amazing story: I tutored a young man, Marty, for a period of time, to prepare him for the SAT. He took the SAT in March of 2007 and did OK - but his scores were a disappointment to him. His average percentile in SAT math, verbal and writing was about 60%. Two weeks later, with very little further prep, he took the ACT. Several weeks went by and then his scores came in. He averaged 90th percentile on all sections (and subsections) of the ACT! These results far exceeded those of his SAT. A big surprise to him - (and me)! It was a perfect example of pupils performing quite differently on these two major exams. Nearly all colleges accept both exams for admission consideration.

As mentioned, there is no specific vocabulary section on the ACT; however, word knowledge will definitely be an asset on your reading comprehension questions.

Let's further discuss the math sections in even a bit more detail now. The ACT math section truly is more of an "achievement" test. That is, if you know your math, you're likely to get many questions correct. With the SAT math, this is not always the case. The SAT may be asking you a math question that requires very basic knowledge but will ask the question in an extremely "tricky" way, thus classifying SAT math questions as "critical thinking" questions rather than simple "achievement" ones. Lots of practice, as always, will help you to succeed on both exams, but especially on the SAT.

There is that "tradeoff" though! The ACT math section includes far more (and more advanced) math topics than does the SAT. So, although many ACT math questions may be "easier" to solve, you must have more math knowledge at your disposal (that is, know more math topics).

As mentioned earlier, for example, there are topics on the ACT math that might include (and usually do), more advanced trigonometry, and logarithms. The SAT avoids these topics. There are many HS juniors who have not yet learned these topics and, thus, have basically no chance for success on them (except by wild guessing, which, as we've mentioned, comes with no penalty on the ACT). However, even though there may be anywhere from, say, 5 to even 15 of these more advanced questions, there might be enough easier questions that the given pupil will handle well and help him receive higher ACT Math grades!

As just mentioned, time is also a large issue on the science section of the ACT. Since there are seven sections to address in 35 minutes, this leaves you with an average of only five minutes per section. Again, this will require lots of practice under timed conditions. Most students struggle with the science section so that a large percentage of ACT test takers are in a "similar boat." The science section does favor careful and thorough readers. Again, going into the test, there is not a lot (if any at all) science that you need to know. It's all right there in the passages. So practice the science under timed conditions, but for sure, the most important sections on both SAT and ACT are reading (verbal) and math with not as much emphasis yet placed on the "writing" (with essay) or "grammar" sections.

Thus, it is, once again, highly recommended that all pupils take both SAT and ACT exams. Only then will you be able to see which is the exam best suited to your style. In addition, you would know on which exam to spend most of your future prep time. It is quite difficult to prepare well for both exams at the same time.

As mentioned, in general, most colleges (if not all) accept equally results on both the SAT and ACT. There are comparison (conversion) charts where scores on both can be compared. Colleges can choose your best results on the

ACT or SAT. Thus, many pupils take either/or both exams - up to three (or even more) times each, seeking to maximize their results.

It is extremely important to contact the admissions department of any college one is interested in applying to. This way, you will be better able to understand the emphasis placed (by each individual college) on SAT/ ACT, Math, Reading, Grammar, and Science results, in addition to how well they adhere to the "Score Choice" Policy of the College Board. Although most colleges have uniformity with regard to the SAT and ACT (universal acceptance of both, choosing your "best" scores, etc.), there will be many individual variations. Some schools may count the "writing" section heavily and some may count it not much at all. There will be numerous other differences from one college to another, so consult each one individually!

When you register for these exams, try to do so as early as possible so you are most likely to get the test site of your choice and will not have to travel extensively. Be aware of all registration procedures. As mentioned, both the ACT and SAT have elaborate websites for you to consult for help and guidance, as well as for test practice. If you desire to receive "live" guidance, you can call either service on the phone. They're very helpful!

When you register, there is no great need to enter any colleges on your application because they can be added later (albeit with a fee). As we've said, one reason not to enter a college name is because, if you do poorly, you can simply not have those scores sent. If you put down the name of a school, they will be sent automatically. Again, consult College Board and ACT for specific rules and regulations, as they may change.

Some of what I discuss here might be current information as of today (winter '13). However, since all rules and procedures are often in flux, it is always important to contact the ACT and SAT and/or the individual colleges on an ongoing basis so that you can keep current.

What about the "SAT Twos?" Well, these are the SAT "Subject Tests." They are given several times a year in many different subject areas. They usually last an hour each and are subject specific. Some colleges have requirements in this area while others do not! Become familiar with the "SAT Twos" as part of your college prep learning. Many pupils never heard of the SAT Twos. It is important for you to investigate as much as you can about the SAT's, the ACT's and the SAT Twos.

Included in the many subject tests that are the SAT Twos is the Math SAT Two - Level One and Level Two. That is, there are two different SAT Two math exams. If the college you plan to attend requests that you take the SAT Two in math, then you must choose the Level One or Two Exam. The Level Two Exam is more rigorous in that it covers more complex topics than does the SAT Two Math Level One. Although questions may be equally challenging on both levels, Level Two covers more advanced topics, such as more from Algebra Two, Trigonometry, and Pre Calculus. By consulting the exam prep books, especially those put out by the College Board (in addition to guidance counselor and/or your math teacher), you can figure out which of the two levels is best for you.

On the SAT II Math exam, you have one hour to do fifty multiple choice questions. Similar formats exist for all of the SAT II subject tests. You can take up to three of these exams on any given Saturday. Please become knowledgeable about them by investigating.

Earlier, we spoke about tutoring. Let's revisit this issue again briefly. Many pupils in their SAT/ACT preparations, as we've said, will want to receive either one on one or small group instruction. There are many many tutors out there. Just how does one go about choosing the appropriate one?

Well, certainly, there is referral. Many parents receive recommendations from friends and neighbors who have had (often) great success with certain tutors. This is likely the best way to go about locating an appropriate tutor. You also want to get some idea of the "track record" of the prospective hiree. Let him or her tell you how his SAT and ACT pupils have done. Get an idea of his approach to the prep process along with practice strategies. In addition, there are some general guidelines which can be helpful in your interview/ selection process. We will revisit the topic of "tutoring" once again in the Chapter "Get Me A Tutor."

We had been discussing SAT vs. ACT. The point here is - give yourself every opportunity to succeed. Here you are being offered two major standardized exams that can be quite critical (or at least very helpful) in the college application process. They are somewhat different and one may favor your style of preparation/achievement over the other. It would be quite wise to take both exams!

Chapter Eleven

The Circle of Success

Let us now discuss the various ingredients of our "Circle of SAT/ACT Success." These ingredients are all necessary to truly bring success to our SAT/ACT Pupils.

First we investigate: "Texts, Workbooks, Practice and Support Materials." This component essentially contains the basic tools necessary for pupil success. There are many books and materials for all the various tests: SAT, SAT II and ACT. As we discussed previously, we have, among them, the "Big Blue" (SAT College Board "Bible"), the "Big Red" (ACT "Bible"), the Barron's grammar book, the box of vocabulary words, the SAT II College Board Books as well as the several support books available (such as "Rocket's Guide to SAT Success," as well as the Princeton Review and Kaplan Practice Texts) that focus on general exam prep for any of these exams. These are the guides available here in 2013 - 2014 and beyond.

This collection of books should remain essentially the same for many years to come - perhaps until the SAT/ACT format might once again be changed (as it was for the SAT in 2005).

Other references, such as Holt's "English Workshop" might serve as useful guides. Even pupil school books, such as math texts, might be needed to help the student review long forgotten formulas and equations.

Mostly however, the major books just mentioned in our earlier chapters, and above, will serve as essential practice material, that when used in an organized and measured way, under the supervision of a tutor, guide or other course leader (or even by the well - disciplined student "on their own") likely will result in very good results.

The next component of our "Circle of SAT/ACT Success" is "Patience, Perseverance and Experience." This is truly a key ingredient. Often, as pupils approach their "exam year" (Grade 11) they know very little about what lies ahead. They often begin in this "know nothing" (or know not much) period. Then they receive an education as to exactly what is contained on these tests. It is truly not until they achieve this awareness that they can truly start making gains. This is the beginning of their path of "experience." It is, as most educational processes in life, a "learning curve." And they enter this curve of "experience" simply by discovering the many ingredients of these tests. With each study session, in fact every time the pupil opens a book and does more examples, works on more strategies, and takes more practice exams, his experience grows and with it so does his score.

Often the pupil takes a practice test (under exam - like conditions) to establish a baseline score. The pupil should take the PSAT - twice. The first time should be in the fall of his sophomore year in High School. Although this is early and the pupil often doesn't have as much knowledge (especially in math) as he'd like to, the exam will give a good reading on "where he's at", and it will add to the experience learning curve.

The pupil goes through the tenth grade, does some studying for the exams and learns a lot in school. Over the summer after tenth grade, the pupil should do lots of preparation for the SAT and ACT. Studying and preparing should be well under way. The problem in 11th grade is that once school begins again, study time for SAT/ACT often becomes more limited as day to day school pressures and responsibilities increase once again. Thus, the summer before grade 11 is a great time to increase his exam prep experience! He takes the PSAT again in his junior year. He is well along the path of the experience curve.

During eleventh grade, the pupil should take the SAT and ACT at least once, and usually at the first time they are given after February (which is usually March or April). In fact, during the 11th grade, the pupil can decide to take the exams well before the March or April dates - there is variation here. By this time, pupils should be pretty much ready for these initial forays into the exams. Taking both exams provides early readings of "real" scores and it also provides more experience for your exam "curve." Since you can usually "dump" poor scores (see Score Choice discussions), there is nearly zero to lose by taking exams several times. Just the practice of taking the "real" exam will add to your experience and very likely your score. You then can take it as many times as you'd like (although at some point scores don't usually move up significantly with repeated sittings - however, you never know!). In fact, you may perform extremely well on an early SAT or ACT, thus significantly decreasing your stress level since you will have a set of good score already "in the bank."

When scores are not to one's satisfaction, "rising" seniors often study significantly in the summer after their junior year at school. They then take the exams at least once more in the fall of their senior year. As far as "SAT Twos," the process is similar although many wait until the very end of junior year (May or June) to take these for the first time as most study up until that point usually would be focused entirely on the "regular" SAT and ACT and not these subject tests. It varies.

This experience that is acquired by our pupils takes patience and perseverance, which are indeed related to one another. To gain all this necessary test "experience" the pupil and all his "support people" must be patient. All students will improve - from the highly talented academically to the academically challenged. Pupils must not be "hard on themselves" but must patiently hang in there! For example, many will go from being virtually clueless on the rules of grammar to becoming expert! Scores can improve by hundreds of points! Pupils need to hang in there and be patient. Math scores improve almost directly with the number of problems one does. We have already mentioned that math knowledge increases as pupils go through the sequence of courses at their respective high schools - Geometry, Algebra I and II, Trigonometry, etc. Scores will increase in this way, and this is one good reason that pupils often wait until spring of their junior year to take these exams "for real." Vocabulary and essay writing skills will also increase with patience and experience.

A new pupil arrived several years ago and his mom came with him to our meeting before the first session, as is sometimes the case. She said to me, in front of her son: "I will not accept less than 750 on any of the SATs." Meanwhile her son received about a 500 on his 10th grade PSAT. The need for patience and reason was definitely indicated there. Comments like these will often doom long - term progress.

Perseverance is the third piece of this circle member. One must continue practicing, analyzing and trying to figure out how to improve. Perseverance is so necessary in assuring that scores will improve over this often year and a half grueling marathon. And they almost always do improve!

Our next circle component is "Early Detection." Early Detection is oh so important here. As it is in life. Diseases that are detected early have such wonderful cure rates. School and social problems, when detected early, have, of course, the best chance for improvement. Why should SAT/ACT issues be any different? When problems are detected early, scores will rise more quickly.

We must seek help for our pupil "as early as possible." For example, the pupil struggling with math or reading needs early intervention to prevent more serious problems later on. This is, of course, a given.

However what about this topic with respect to SAT/ACT? Early detection means that the pupil should take the PSAT in tenth grade. Do not wait until eleventh grade (although some schools "do not allow" 10th graders to take the PSAT). In addition, the pupil could benefit from a Kaplan/Princeton Review full SAT/ACT assessment, as we've discussed earlier. By taking the PAST and/or a "Kaplan-type" practice SAT, the pupil will be provided with feedback quite early in the process - certainly with enough time to secure the help needed to increase scores. For example, the tenth grader takes the PSAT in October of this, his sophomore year. His grammar and math scores are unexpectedly low and his Kaplan practice test essay is a lowly total of 5. He now knows where he stands and corrective action can begin as soon as possible! Know where you stand - early - then work hard to improve your weak points. This is "Early Detection."

Along with Early Detection is "Needs Assessment." When your performance is evaluated early in the process, you will know where you'll need to focus your studying. If your critical reading PSAT is 65 (650) and your grammar result is 45 (450) then you can ease off on the reading section and focus lots of your precious 11th grade study time on the grammar section . . . or perhaps the essay writing. In any case, your "Needs Assessment" will help you to shape your study game plan. Without the diagnosis, the treatment plan will truly be confusing.

Moving around our "Circle of Success" we arrive at "Self-Education" as our next stop. This piece is truly quite important in our whole situation. The pupil needs to work hard on his own. Even if he has a private tutor or is a member of some kind of prep class there is a great need for "self-study." It is during this time that real progress is often made. For example, a pupil scores quite low on the tenth grade PSAT writing/grammar section. The problem has been detected early and a need has been assessed. The pupil now begins her process of self-education. Under the possible guidance of a tutor or class, she obtains material that will help her to learn the many rules of grammar which contain some of what needs to be mastered for the SAT/ACT in this section. If there is no "guru" to help her, she will learn the names of the best grammar "bibles" to use for study for her self -education via books like this one (the one you are currently reading) where these "best" books are suggested.

At this point the true self - studying process takes over. The pupil begins to learn all the grammar rules in detail and via practice with the appropriate materials now, grammar understanding begins to improve as do the scores. Hard work and more practice will enhance the pupil's score ascent on his exams.

The same "Self - Education" process is applied to the reading comprehension, math, science (ACT only), essay writing and vocabulary sections of the exam. Yes, do seek help if you can, but self - education and self study are how scores rise best, often quite rapidly!

The parent also is required to get involved with this "Self - Education" idea. The parent can help her child by knowing all that she can about the eleventh grade year. The parent can help her child by trying to become an expert in the components of and study methods for these big exams. As a result, parents thus will be able to help more effectively if their children have questions to be answered or guidance to be sought. Parents should know about test sites, testing dates, registration methods - in short, anything that can help their children succeed on these college entrance exams. Here in 2012 - 13 the College Board has books and websites (mentioned elsewhere) available that will help pupils and parents learn and plan their strategies during each respective grade level starting with grade 9. Thus, parents are involved in the Circle at both the "Self - Education" and the "Parent (PTA) Participation" components of the Circle.

After each exam that is taken, more self - education opportunities are available as the SAT and ACT "people" often distribute (or sometimes do, depending on the month you sit for the exam) detailed analyses of your particular exam (usually must be ordered). More study . . . more chance for higher grades! Self - education also occurs with regard to, e.g., "test taking strategies" - i.e., guessing (should you guess? . . . if so, when?), pacing, etc. The many strategy books available will help in these exam strategies.

As we continue touring our exam Circle of Success, we next stop at "Site-Selection, Logistics of Registration and Exam Calendar." Basically, you need to know details regarding your registration procedures. You should obtain booklets from your guidance department for both the SAT and ACT. These booklets, released by the SAT and ACT "people" explain almost everything you need to know about these exams. They are necessary readings, especially for the tenth grader who is completely new to the process. The College Board and ACT websites also contain this information.

It is essential to know the dates of all exams so that you can plan your schedule effectively. For example, many pupils take the exams initially in March (or April depending on exam and particular year) of their junior year and then again for a second or even third time. Knowledge of dates is essential in your planning. As mentioned earlier, a few students even take the exams earlier than the spring (of grade 11), and this practice is no longer a rarity.

Pupils must become familiar with some of the SAT scheduling issues: for example, one cannot take an "SAT II" exam on the same day as the "regular" SAT. Or, the maximum number of SAT II's one can take on a given day is three. Or, what happens if one becomes ill before or during an SAT or ACT? These and other "tricky" questions may require answers at some point.

In addition to being "up" on the dates, you must register early enough so that you will likely get a site at, perhaps, your home school, or, at the very least, a site close to home or somewhere where you know you'd be comfortable.

Many pupils often have similar questions such as: Can I take an SAT II on a Sunday? This and other questions (many others that will arise on an individual basis) need to be answered and they will be (often with help from your guidance counselor, your tutor, your school or your own networking). And just the fact that these questions are being answered will help scores to increase.

As far as the registration process itself, it is all clearly indicated in the booklets we've spoken about (those available at your guidance office) as well as online at the appropriate websites. In fact, if somehow you miss a deadline, there are ways of registering as a "stand - by" candidate, thus allowing you a "second chance" to sit for the exam. There are also other alternate registration methods. So the wise candidate will sit down and carefully map out his time frame for test taking.

As we travel around the Circle of Success, we arrive at "Networking with the World". As in many other areas of life, networking is extremely important. Via networking you can reach out and get many wonderful ideas that might never occur to you. There are many students and parents who've successfully navigated the choppy waters of the SAT/ACT. They can serve as your guides. There are your friends, your relatives, your teachers, the guidance and college - advisory staff, etc. Touch base with representatives from Kaplan and Princeton Review; with local tutors; read the advisory books and manuals. Get lists of tutors from your local high school guidance department. In other words, reach out and network with as many sources as you can! Your comfort level, confidence, and ultimately, your SAT/ACT score will all increase dramatically. I, for example, have lots of success with many students whom I tutor. The following year I often receive calls to tutor their siblings and/or friends. Referral to successful practice is often so critical to exam success!

The reason I have a separate component on our Circle of Exam Success for something as obvious as practice (see "Practice, Practice, Practice Plus") is that it is likely one of the most important ingredients in the entire discussion. Without it you truly will not progress very far. Like most good things, hard work and practice will help you realize your dreams and achieve your goals. Pupils who do not practice math, for example, who do not learn how to solve those difficult problems, who do not learn the fundamentals that they lack, will not make those seemingly miraculous gains that truly are possible. For the real estate agent it is location, location, location - for the SAT/ACT high achiever it is Practice, Practice, and Practice Plus.

Let us discuss "Parent (PTA) Participation." Remember, we are trying to enhance SAT/ACT scores as much as we can! Here is yet another important ingredient of our circle. Parent participation simply means that the parent gets involved in the high school via participation in the PTA (sometimes known as PTO). In other words, the parent attends meetings at school involving these organizations. Often, in the fall, schools host a "College Night" for students and parents - at which representatives from large numbers of colleges are in attendance. Pupils and parents can come and get valuable information about hundreds of these colleges. They can ask questions and receive advice and guidance. They can ask college representatives for details on SAT/ACT procedures, preparation and strategies. Different colleges have different requirements - not only regarding SAT/ACT - but also as far as the "SAT Twos" are concerned. For example, some college may request an SAT II in Math; others may desire that the pupil take this one hour subject test in Science, etc.

Parents can attend the lecture and presentations that are usually available in their child's particular school district, or they can attend presentations privately. For example, I often present evening workshops at the local library to parents (and students) with titles such as: "How to Help Your Child Succeed on the SAT and ACT" - ("How to Survive and Thrive Magnificently on the SAT and ACT"). During these (and other) presentations, involved participants pick up more essential information that can be an invaluable aid to exam success. Parents should attend workshops like these in their local communities.

We see that involved parents can truly provide a lot of support, guidance, and knowledge to their children. More about parent involvement soon.

Our next stop on our Circle tour is "College Networking." During the junior year in high school, pupils often make visits to campuses of colleges they might be interested in attending. This is truly an exciting way to get familiar with the ABC's of college life - including application process, financial aid detail, coursework, living accommodations, etc. It is also a wonderful chance for pupils and parents to ask questions about exam requirements (SAT/ACT) and to pick up further ideas and strategies that will help pupils with the entire exam - related process. It is similar to a "college night" in that one can accumulate many new ideas and strategies!

In addition, the college touring provides a great opportunity for the family to "bond," come together and share in the excitement and challenge of this new phase in the lives of both the parent and the child. So on our "Circle of SAT Success," pupils and parents not only gain information on exam prep (which usually translates into more SAT/ACT points) but also enjoy the many benefits of sharing this family challenge.

"Test Logistics" is the next stop on our "Circle of Success." Remember, the "Circle" is the graphic summary of the most important ingredients that go into the making of SAT/ACT success!

"Test Logistics" is extremely important. You must know, for example, whether you should "guess" if you have no idea of an answer. Is there a "penalty?" Should you ever/never leave blanks on your answer sheet? What must you know about timing and "answer gridding?" Knowledge of the answers to these questions will often help provide great increases in test scores.

On the SAT, there are minor penalties for wrong answers so when one does not have any idea of an answer, it is usually best to leave answer bubbles blank. However, if one can eliminate just one answer choice, it may pay to "guess." Math (SAT) grid - ins carry no penalty for wrong answers. For grammar and verbal test questions, many experts say not to leave blanks since most pupils can usually narrow down the field of choices.

On the ACT there is never any penalty for wrong answers (so never leave blanks on the ACT). The point is, via your readings and conversations, you will become aware that "guessing," "filling in blanks," and more, are important strategies with which to be familiar. These strategies can translate into increases of literally tens to over hundreds of points. You need to formulate a philosophy in this logistical area.

Just as a jockey or track star must be ever - aware of pacing and timing, so must the SAT/ACT "athlete." Pacing and timing are extremely important. Practice in and familiarity with these areas can reap huge benefits. Let's repeat some ACT information as an illustration of this point. On the ACT verbal (reading) section, there are four reading selections and the test - taker has 35 minutes to read them and answer all of the questions. That means that the pupil must average eight minutes and 45 seconds per selection. This is extremely important information. I had one pupil who was an excellent reader but was totally oblivious to this time issue (before we began our work together). She did quite well on passages one and two but because she took so much time, she was "destroyed" on passages three and four. She took the ACT again a month later and armed with all her knowledge about timing, she did remarkably well. The time to rehearse this all important skill is during your practice sessions or practice tests. Always have the "clock" in mind - as if you were a jockey in the Kentucky Derby and the "pace" were super - important! As we have discussed, this aspect of SAT/ACT prep is quite critical. As far as "extended" time, if you are allowed this accommodation, be sure you apply for it far in advance. Also, if you have an "accommodation," research into application procedure - either via school guidance or via College Board (or ACT) request. Your guidance department should fully explain procedures. So we must know that something like "Test Logistics" can also be of critical import to bolstering your exam results!

The "Main Course" is our next stop in our "Circle of Success." The "Main Course" is simply a summary of all of the truly essential components of the exams - the actual subject matter - the "nitty gritty." We have already discussed most of these ingredients in much detail in the previous pages. However, since the "Circle" is a summary, let's reiterate some of the high points. Many points have already been discussed in detail so for some we will not review them in their entirety. Thus, for fuller discussion, simply refer back to the appropriate section in the book.

First we have the verbal or reading comprehension section. On both SAT and ACT there are several reading passages. The SAT includes explicit vocabulary questions while the ACT does not. There are some other differences between the two exams in this verbal area, which have been discussed.

On both exams you must be aware of time limits and you must thus pace accordingly. Practice will certainly improve your results but practice must incorporate careful analysis in order to eliminate errors and learn how to choose between similar answers. For the SAT, vocabulary lists (cards, etc.) should be memorized in order to increase word knowledge.

Next in our "Main Course" agenda is the essay. Pupils eventually need practice under time pressure to be sure that their essay - writing skills are of high quality. They can use any structure for their essay; however, the 5 paragraph essay format can provide the security of a set pattern. Pupils usually refer to evidence from history, current events, readings, and personal experience to support their viewpoints. The references to academics and current events are employed especially on the SAT essay. SAT topics are not quite as "straightforward" as those on the ACT. Pupils should always receive feedback on their practice essays from teachers, parents, friends and/or tutors. There is much reading (in the Prep Manuals) that can be done by pupils regarding essay writing strategies that will help to hone this skill. A brief outline is always an excellent pre - writing skill.

Regarding "Main Course" grammar, we have the Grammar/Writing section on the SAT and the "English" section on the ACT. They are quite similar. We've discussed the minor differences. Pupils learn the rules of grammar (many do not know them well at first) via tutoring and use of grammar rule books and practice materials. They continue their practicing and eventually scores do improve, often dramatically. As always, they learn that they are tested by several different types of questions and they become familiar with each one of them.

The final part of the "Main Course" is the math section. The SAT and ACT math sections can differ significantly and thus it is often recommended that the pupil take both exams. Many of the topics are similar but the ACT covers many more components of the HS math curriculum (including trigonometry). The SAT math seems much "trickier" and more challenging but doesn't cover quite as many topics. Again, on both, practice is the key to success. Take both exams and see which one may be more suited to your math skills.

Our next stop around our Circle of Success is "www.Collegeboard.com" and "ACTstudent.org." These websites are "must - sees" and "must - uses" for our SAT/ACT candidate and his or her parent. These sites contain an enormous amount of invaluable information for exam success!

On the SAT site there are separate areas for students, parents and administrators. It is essential that you sign up for both sites (SAT and ACT) and explore all that they have to offer.

As far as the College Board and ACT websites, it is critical not only to be "surfing" them constantly but also to be aware of the fact that there are these two major exams, that you should absolutely take both and that you should be aware that multiple sittings of the two (if necessary) can likely help you in your application process.

The sites offer information regarding test prep, financial aid, individual college news, how to choose the right college, applying to college and test admission data. They further offer information on study strategies, career planning and other extremely critical tidbits for exam success. There are sections of "frequently asked questions," there are even student blogs that help pupils get a feel for the entire college application process. You can retrieve your exam results on these sites. The sites are absolutely essential components of exam prep.

If necessary, "Referrals" will be made. In other words, assuming that there is going to be a need for other than the usual methods of assistance, channels have been set up (throughout this book) for you to discover how to obtain a "referral" to the appropriate expert - be it a math or science tutor, a special education evaluation, a speech therapist, a psychologist, social worker, psychiatrist, general practitioner, dentist, lawyer, or whomever. The Circle of Success is almost complete. Soon, its pieces will magically link together and begin spinning. Lights will shine, bells will sound, and whistles will be heard. It soon will be time to celebrate and rejoice! Notice the aforementioned "melting together" of the various inputs from our Circle.

I hope our tour around the "Circle of Success" has been informative. If one employs all parts of the Circle in SAT/ACT planning, then exam results truly will be quite satisfactory for students at all levels of achievement.

Chapter Twelve

Get Me A Tutor!

This chapter deals with the hiring of a tutor. In the book, we have discussed various forms of assistance for the pupil. We have mentioned "one on one" and small and large group situations. In this chapter we focus on the hiring of a "one on one" tutor, which, when financially feasible, I find gives maximum benefit. I have been a "one on one" tutor for almost thirty - eight years. I have also done "small groups" and "full-size" classes. I write from major experience.

In addition, I would add that this chapter is necessary reading for parents since they are the ones who will do the hiring of the tutor. However, pupils also can benefit from reading here.

I have been tutoring math, SAT, ACT, and other subjects privately now for over 38 years. The one on one situation provides an especially unique opportunity for the tutor to really get deeply involved in the learning process - to really examine its dynamics. Tutoring, like most other services, comes in assorted varieties with respect to prices, quality, and effectiveness. Since some parents are not familiar with the process of hiring, monitoring and evaluating a tutoring program, I present this chapter. Thus, this chapter has a very important purpose. However, it becomes truly of great significance when viewed from another angle as well.

We have discussed throughout this book many of the practices and attitudes that parents and students must possess in order to reach that ultimate goal of pupil success. This chapter will touch on many of these same components, since the tutor is ideally one who also successfully touches on most of the ingredients in our Circle of Success. Thus, reading this chapter will not only help you to select an appropriate tutor for your child (if that is what you need) but it will also serve to reinforce and review for you some of those very important ideas we've covered already in the book. Also, hiring and monitoring a tutor often parallels, in some ways, the hiring of other support services that you may need for your child - from doctor to psychologist to dentist. In any case, please read this chapter carefully, for it will definitely help you to put things together even more effectively.

This next section is for tutors "in general." However, the principles are similar and can be applied to the SAT tutor as well.

Now that school is in full swing (or beginning), the subject of "tutoring" often arises. Just what qualities go into making a good (or great) tutor for your children? What does one look for in choosing a tutor? - what qualities are important? How does one know if the relationship is a positive one, and that your child is growing, both academically and emotionally?

A good tutor should possess some characteristic work traits. He (or she) must be courteous and polite at all times and in all situations. A tutor must be reliable and responsible, always on time - never beginning too early and never (except in extremely rare instances) late. Since he will also hopefully serve as a role model, he will have impeccable manners and professional dress.

Often a tutor comes to your attention via recommendation from a satisfied friend. This of course is the best method of selection. You have a trusted friend who has been a contented customer - great! Hopefully, the tutor will be a "nice fit" for your child as well.

At times you may answer an ad from the newspaper or a flyer. You will get certain vibes on the phone from the potential tutor. Get the essential information: cost, time (length) of session, availability, your place or mine, references, tutor background (education, work history, current assignment), tutor's philosophy of education, etc. Remember that this is your (or your child's) education that you are talking about - what else could be more important? Get as much information as you can in order to formulate a wise decision on your choice for a tutor. A good tutor will have a set price and does not negotiate like a car salesperson hot on a deal. A good tutor will not <u>guarantee</u> results or tell you exactly how many sessions you will need (impossible before even meeting with the student for the very first time). Yes it is true that high SAT/ACT results cannot be guaranteed but the tutor usually can discuss some sort of statistical track record that he possesses. Also, it should be explained that over the long process that extends from PSAT to SAT/ACT, scores usually do improve. Over the following paragraphs, we'll discuss how the aforementioned philosophy of education, as well as other factors, should be weighed in choosing a tutor, as well as in deciding if the chosen person is the very best one for your child.

Your potential choice should have a solid set of references if called upon to supply them. Some appropriate references would, of course, be satisfied clients and/or school supervisors. For example, a high school math teacher should supply the names of his department chair and/or his principal. Sometimes, in speaking to a really great professional, one can almost feel that they are good, and might not even need a reference. It is, however, always good to totally check someone out before hiring them.

Often the tutor is a well - known veteran in the community who comes with superb word of mouth references. Eventually, some amount of trust will be necessary. Many parents, again, want to know, immediately, how many sessions it will take for Johnny to secure a 90 average in math. Again, answers to questions like these are truly impossible to give. One cannot possibly assign a deadline or time schedule to understanding and learning concepts and ideas. In our discussion of the "Circle of Success," we emphasize that success takes "Patience, Perseverance and Experience" on the part of both pupil and parent. Improvement can be a slow process and often factors other than the number of sessions are involved. For example, as pupil confidence builds, improvement often comes in leaps and bounds.

In getting a recommendation from a person's work site, you can get an objective picture of a person's job performance, habits and work ethic. If a teacher has a good reputation in the workplace, chances are that that person will satisfy many of your tutoring needs as well. Other helpful "bullets" in the recommendation "résumé" include a person's degrees and experiences, number of years in teaching, number of years in tutoring, awards won, and publications, if any. After all, you are conducting a job search for a truly most important position in your life. You are a casting director and need a "Star" to perform in your upcoming Broadway extravaganza - and you want it to be a hit show!

Again, you will often know the tutor well - because of his reputation in the community - or you may have already used him for another one of your children. If you do not have access to a tutor, you can often find leads from the guidance department at your child's school (or another school nearby). Schools often provide phone numbers of available tutors that parents can call and interview. For SAT/ACT enhancement tutoring, at the initial session, the tutor often gets the student totally educated to the "ins and outs" of the exams.

Usually, the initial session is really a planning, strategy or "getting to know you" meeting, where teacher and student meet, greet and assess. A good relationship with positive rapport always is the aim of this initial session. It is the job of the instructor to help her pupil to feel at ease and lower the barriers, fences and defenses that many pupils have built to "defend" against successful learning. Very often it is these "barriers" to learning and not always academic deficiencies that prevent success in school. It is critical that these barriers be lowered. Of course, for many pupils, there is, additionally, a lack of technical skill in the given subject area and much remediation and practice may be indicated. However, for most, there is the combination of <u>both</u> of these issues - cognitive (facts and actual subject material) and affective (mainly psychological/emotional issues) that must be worked on in the (usually) one-to-one tutoring situation. Thus, putting any "deadline" for success on the entire tutoring process will surely result in anxiety, stress and eventually failure.

As far as the "technical deficiencies" that we speak of, there will be pupils who are obviously gifted, let's say, for example, in math. There will be other pupils who arrive to you (the tutor) with quite poor math skills. Of course you will work with the two in completely different ways, and although both will likely improve, the immediate or short - term expectations will differ for the two as well. For the pupil who does quite poorly on the PSAT or SAT (achieving say, a math grade of "310" (out of a possible 800) - quite low) - the instructor will have to slowly remediate (at times major) math deficits. Here I speak of the SAT and PSAT. ACT equivalents could have been used as well. Use of conversion charts will help to equate the SAT and ACT scores! Most pupils with very low math scores will require large amounts of training in "basic skills". So quite slowly the remediation process begins. It may take a while but improvement will occur. Patience and perseverance are required. Miracles are directly proportional to the amount of hard work expended by the pupil.

For the advanced math student the methodology is different. The student who scores above the 90th percentile (say an SAT score of over 650) is not going to require much remediation. Here, in this case, we must work on lots of practice problems (especially with the problems of high difficulty) in order to get scores to rise.

Thus, in working with pupils, there are different methods that are used with students of varied abilities. Parents and pupils need to understand this. There needs to be a level of patience and satisfaction with academic growth, even if it progresses at a slower pace than what they desire. The same idea holds true for the other parts of the exam - reading, grammar and essay writing (on both the ACT and SAT).

It is the pupil's responsibility to do his homework - i.e., work on the practice problems and memorize vocabulary words. However, at times, parents will need to intervene (as per tutor report), as usual, to see to it that pupils are working responsibly to improve their grades.

So, we can say that we hope grades will improve, but along with improved grades we seek an improvement in attitude as well - pupil motivation, dedication, and interest in learning and improving. Attitude change can be slow - it can be quick. It can take years, it can take days. It is one of the jobs of the tutor to improve academic performance, but an attitudinal change (and perhaps positive lifestyle change), where necessary, is often a collateral and wonderful bonus result of the tutoring experience.

In this book it is our goal to improve SAT/ACT scores - often dramatically. And this has happened quite often in our tutoring practice. Part of improvement does depend on the motivation factor. It can be the difference that will result in gains of literally hundreds of points. Often pupils need to be motivated to become motivated. But the result of this enhanced desire will be enormous.

We spoke of the youngster who began treating math practice as a "game" - it actually became a fun activity for him; he did the practice instead of watching TV or using the computer. His scores rose dramatically.

One young lady I worked with (discussed earlier) became ultra - motivated because at that point she truly wanted to increase her score enough to gain entry to a certain college. A good math student to begin with, she observed her math score rise from 470 on the PSAT to 730 on the SAT. And it resulted from lots of practice along with much learning of required math formulas and procedures that she had forgotten or had never learned. She is now a tutor for the Princeton Review - and is in her senior year at a wonderful college. She caught "motivation fever." One after another, pupils often gain this motivational attitude and it drives them to put in the necessary practice time. If it is lacking, it is up to the teacher/tutor or even the parent to try to affect it. It is just so important!

In just one year or two our pupil will be heading off to college. The skills she has learned under your tutelage - motivation, study habits, discipline - will stay with her and help her throughout high school, college, graduate school and life.

Your home or mine? Some tutors will come to your home (and charge for travel time and transportation in many cases) while others will have you visit theirs (or their offices). The key is comfort and environmental suitability. It is critical that the tutoring location be totally quiet and conducive to learning. It must have superb lighting, as well as all of the other necessary accoutrements: comfortable desk and chairs, pleasant atmosphere, and, again, be educationally appropriate (from all of the proper angles). I have seen tutors working in homes with TV sets blaring, parents and siblings screaming, tremendous outside noise, cramped desk areas, horrible lighting and other ridiculously unprofessional situations. The effective tutor will not tolerate operations of this manner, and, hopefully, you will see to it that these situations are not allowed to exist.

Remember that it may have taken years for your child to have developed a negative attitude (if it exists - although often this is not an issue). Don't expect it to necessarily melt away in mere months. On the other hand, the problem may very well melt away in weeks or even days. If the pupil becomes motivated and really begins to care and work really hard, yes change can even happen "overnight."

Your tutor should be an academic (subject area) specialist in the chosen area of need. He should be totally comfortable with the subject matter in question - hopefully having taught the specific subject (and related ones) for many years. As far as SAT/ACT, some tutors (and courses) focus only on math; others focus only on verbal while still others present all sections of the exam. So for these exams you're looking for expertise in math skills, verbal skills, or both. In addition, most instructors, as we've said, can provide you with information regarding their performance track record.

However, first and foremost, the tutor should be an excellent teacher - a person supremely capable of conveying the material in question to his charges in a well-understood, pleasant, motivational and efficient manner. If he is an "Albert Einstein" in his field, yet is unable to effectively transfer or teach his field of expertise, he's just a "name" to you, and this you do not need! The tutor, as mentioned, hopefully also has taught subjects related to the one in question as well. When one is teaching a certain level of math, for example, it helps greatly for the teacher to know the previous level, those subsequent to it and even related fields such as physics and biology. The broader one's knowledge base, the better tutor one is. This description is for tutoring in general. For SAT/ACT instruction, the tutor should be quite familiar with the structure and makeup of the exam. He should be knowledgeable of the latest changes that come along, should attend College Board presentations and be in touch with all related information. The tutor (or course) will have much appropriate practice material that accurately reflects exam questions and is tailored to your child's individual needs.

At the tutoring location, it is important that the teacher be equipped with all the necessary "tools of the trade." In math, for example, it is ruler, protractor, calculator (regular, scientific _and_ especially, graphing), compass, colored pencils (for diagrams), graph paper, scrap paper (the life blood of tutoring), all the necessary textbooks, review books and other essential resources. The successful tutor is always prepared far in advance of the lesson.

The SAT/ACT tutor (or class) does not only provide instruction in the required material. He should provide so much more. The tutor either will refer you to sources that will help you navigate the process or will provide the guidance himself.

This guidance information is crucial in helping your child succeed. The tutor, with all of his connections, knowledge, and networking experience, will be sure that you and your child are aware of registration deadlines, exam dates and locations, procedures for filing for extra time (if available to your child), strategies for exam day prep, as well as prep during the days before the exam. He will familiarize you with the important websites, phone numbers, college information, methods of obtaining your scores and supplementary material after each exam. The tutor will help you to interpret your scores and compare ACT results to those from the SAT. He will tell you all about the SAT Twos, about which ones to take and when to take them.

At times, pupils realize, at the last minute, that their registration procedure was not done correctly. It can be arranged that they go "standby," a procedure which greatly increases the likelihood of their gaining admission to the exam. So yes, the tutor you hire or the course your child takes could provide significantly more help than simply subject matter instruction. As we have seen there often are many intangibles that affect SAT/ACT results. Recently, one of my pupils expressed so much anxiety about exam results that he was indeed "afraid" to get his score and trusted me so much that he asked that I retrieve the scores for him. This is often some of that extra sensitivity that you would want to see in the tutor for your child.

The master tutor is a master psychologist. He spots the problems that are interfering with learning and must often solve them by creative methods, because direct attempts may often fail. For example, tension, stress, and anxiety often "melt away" by using math puzzles, games and other positive strategies with appropriate students. One book that I have written is based on this concept which I have been successfully using for the past 38 years. As discussed, it is entitled "Just Let Me Survive Today:" A Primer in Classroom Management and Motivation. The tutor knows which buttons to press and how and when to press them. He is a master of guidance, replete with unlimited understanding and patience.

I tutored one pupil who had developed an eating disorder related to pressures from eleventh grade - from parents, exams, college application stresses, etc. I have seen parents put enormous pressure on their children and children "break" or nearly break due to these stresses. Each case needs to be handled on an individual basis. Again, it is this sensitivity and ability to diagnose trouble that you often seek and should covet in your child's instructor.

The tutor has established a good relationship with his pupil. The pupil feels very comfortable with his one on one partner and very often even looks forward to the meetings. The student self esteem and sense of power is growing. Success is not far off. But don't rush it - "Nurture it . . . and it will come." Again, this discussion is based on the qualifications of all tutors - not simply those that instruct SAT and ACT!

We have discussed texts and other reference materials. Be advised that the ideal tutor will have a list of the best reference materials for student use. The tutor will allow you to either purchase them from him, or retrieve them from Barnes and Noble, Amazon, etc. The books have proven highly effective in the SAT/ACT prep procedures. Now I will present some more general guidelines for tutors of just about any subject.

The tutor knows the texts that are most appropriate for the particular course. He may decide to use the one that the student uses in school, or he may decide to use one of his own choices - or some review books or some standardized test material. However, the tutor will have (via experience with this subject or by research) knowledge of all the various texts available for the course and thus will be in a great position to make the wisest choice possible.

Next on your "tutor checklist" is organization. The excellent tutor (or course) insures that pupils put a great emphasis on organizational skills. Here is yet another reason why the one on one tutor is optimum. He can more easily zero in on and check pupil work and homework in detail. In a large (or even small) class this checking process is often incomplete. For SAT/ACT, e.g., I have my pupils write all their work directly in the various workbooks, be sure that they check all answers, require that they keep organized computerized lists of vocabulary words, often time themselves (with stopwatch) during practice, chart the results, and show all work. Most classes are too large to effect these detailed checking strategies.

By helping pupils to organize, the tutor guides them to be more careful on the actual exams and in addition he helps them to maximize the efficiency of their practice sessions. Once again I now add some general organizational commentary that applies to all tutoring situations.

The tutor would like to inculcate good organizational skills as well as good study habits in her pupil. Often pupils are poorly organized - their notebooks are completely out of order, the pages are falling out, creased and wrinkled. They need to get organized! The competent tutor will see to it that notebooks are fully rearranged and monitored for maintenance. The parent should also become an active participant in the monitoring of her child's notebook, being certain that it remains in tip-top organizational condition, for this is often the first step toward a successful academic situation.

As your child gets older you have to decide just how much supervision you might need to inject into his situation. You need to strike a healthy balance: on one hand you need to unobtrusively check and monitor his progress, supply guidance and offer emotional support versus on the other hand you completely micromanage his study and academic work. You need to know your child and his needs, or get to know them. You may need to employ trial and error to discover these needs.

Basically, the non SAT/ACT student should establish a well-set up loose-leaf binder (for easily removable and movable notes) that is stocked with reinforcements, and is organized into sections - homework, class work, etc., for each subject. Why is this of such critical importance? At exam time, you want to be able to help your child go through, in a very detailed manner, the class notes that will reflect that which is on the exam. You'd be surprised to know how important this is. Many teachers take their exams directly from pupil notes. Some highlight in the notes exactly what is going to be on the exam. At the very least, the notes usually contain information on exam dates and structures. They can, if in good shape, give golden insights into upcoming exams, as well as often help out with everyday note - taking procedures. In monitoring your child's progress in tutoring, be aware of this important area. Be aware, as mentioned earlier, that many teachers provide pupils with study guides and "review sheets" that are of major assistance in focusing pupils on the study process. Tutors of course need access to these valuable aids. At times, pupils "forget to bring them" to their tutoring session, which of course must be avoided. Pupils always need to be prepared for their sessions with appropriate texts and study materials.

You (the tutor) do want to help your pupil adjust to (and deal with) the given teacher at school, but before you get involved in this whole process, you may want to advise the parent alone to do most of the questioning and networking with the pupil's school.

With reference to the SAT/ACT situation, there is not a critical need for you (the parent) to network with the child's school - with some exceptions. Many schools offer some form of SAT/ACT support, be it via formal classes or via extra "lab" sessions or via during or after - school tutoring sessions. Some schools hire companies (like the Kaplan company) to administer practice exams or even to perform all types of tutoring. Your child's guidance counselor should be able to provide your child with support on the entire college application process. So it absolutely can help if you research all of the resources that are offered by the school your son or daughter attends!

We are about ready to continue our discussion of "motivation," yet another critical factor that the tutor deals with.

When it comes to the SAT/ACT situation, motivation is generally not as large a problem as during the "regular" school year. By this time (11th grade), many pupils are motivated by high school graduation, college applications and their futures. However, many pupils still have trouble with their motivation. Or, they might "think" they're motivated but do not translate their desire into action. This ability to motivate is an excellent quality possessed by a tutor.

Some pupils are very responsible with their SAT/ACT assignments while other pupils do not carefully do their SAT/ACT "homework." Some don't do it at all, others "fake it" (by copying answers from answer guides). Some are just overwhelmed by their regular schoolwork (which is why summer and holidays are great times for SAT/ACT exam prep). Some are lazy (do not prepare vocabulary lists e.g.), some have every kind of excuse and some just require "injections" of spirit, "pep" talks and ongoing work on their desires. It is the tutor's role to try to make this motivation "happen." How? Well the experienced tutor knows how important this aspect of learning is and will keep seeking ways to enhance motivation. The tutor will tailor it to his individual student. Again, however, we place it on our list of qualities to look for in your instructor. We describe briefly some of the methods that are used by various instructors. And the best of the instructors are constantly searching for various methods to motivate.

What about this motivation? Many pupils lack this essential learning component. How does one get it? This is within the realm of the experienced and expert tutor. In the tutoring sessions, the creative methods of the tutor will focus attention on this issue. Through conversations with the pupil, both direct and indirect, and by employing creative techniques, the tutor will try to enhance the motivation and desire in the student. He will try to get the student to "care," to find a reason to study and learn . . . because it is "fun," because the pupil wants to achieve a certain goal that requires good grades, or for those idealistic "pure learning" reasons. Whatever! The student will have achieved a component <u>critical</u> to success in the land of academia: MOTIVATION! The parent should be extremely pleased when this day approaches (assuming it's not yet here) and should go out and celebrate big time when it actually arrives. The successful tutor knows the significance of this achievement.

The parent should be observant that the tutor is working on this issue and that the instructor covets its achievement. The parent should watch that the development of feelings and thoughts like those just mentioned are primary in the planning agenda and in the philosophy of our valuable tutoring person. Motivation is of course a key element in the tutoring process. However, many of your students may already be motivated; that's why they're seeing you. Others may just need some temporary help - for the upcoming test or for the SAT/ACT. In other words, pupils will be coming to tutoring for a great number of different reasons - not only to work on their motivation.

Once more it is the expert tutor's job to take this developing motivation and to nurture it and to help it grow into the wonderful "garden" that will help our pupil succeed on the SAT, ACT, in college and in life. Most of these juniors (11th graders) have the beginnings (or fully developed condition) of "motivation fever". They simply need to know how to cultivate it or enhance it.

In developing this critical factor of motivation, the creative tutor may employ a "bag of tricks." The parent should watch for evidence of creativity of this sort - that will lead to the achievement of a highly motivated pupil. For some, this "bag of tricks" contains incentive prizes and rewards that will motivate pupils. Sometimes a "prize" (like a CD, a basketball or a pack of baseball cards) or a math "game" might serve to help motivate a young student.

Many older kids (your SAT/ACT group) and adult learners often become fully motivated and they might be "turned on" simply by a stimulating lesson (or desire to do well on an entrance exam of some sort). The point is, the development of motivation and desire is of critical import, the parent should be aware of this and in touch with it, and the tutor must use his "mystical" creative power to formulate it in his students. The tutor must get to know his pupil well enough that he will know just what formula it might take to "reach" this particular pupil. It may be a connection with sports; the tutor would then connect his lessons to a sports theme. For example, one of my Yankee fan tutees was able to memorize the times tables by reference to players' uniform numbers. Another pupil was a rabid NASCAR fan and he used drivers' car numbers as an aid in memorizing mathematically - related items.

Many pupils are avid sports fans and this connection can provide wonderful examples of role models who have overcome all odds to succeed. Basketball buffs know that when the game is "on the line", one foul shot can mean the difference between victory and defeat. And success in foul shooting is directly proportional to the amount of student practice time. No practice time means increased likelihood of errors on the field and on the exam. This and hundreds of other examples from the sports world can help motivate many pupils. Of course, non-sports fans can be motivated in a similar way using the hobby or material they might be interested in: It might be computers - and then the instructor would spice his lessons with a computer angle - perhaps delve into the Internet and send e-mails back and forth. The point is, most pupils, young and old, have "hooks" that the tutor can take advantage of in hastening the learning process. These activities often create pupil excitement and this enthusiasm may very well spill into school and home life, creating positive results for all concerned. Again, these little bits of creative thinking strategies are not needed to the same extent by all pupils. However, the expert teacher knows that creative instruction always enhances learning for every pupil. The tutor you are searching for is one who can motivate pupils by employing creative methods that are often expertly tailored to the unique pupil at hand.

The tutoring process has begun. How does a parent know, really know, if the work is progressing satisfactorily? This similar question can be asked about the child's school progress. Well, the first procedure the parent should do is to communicate with the child. In other words, talk to your son or daughter. Ask them how they feel about the tutor and about the entire process. This is an initial (albeit critical) step for the concerned parent to take. Usually, the parent will get a "feel" for the situation via this line of questioning. However, just because your child "loves" the tutor does not necessarily mean that all is going well. The reverse is true as well. But it sure is a positive sign in your evaluation process. This questioning should be ongoing. Talk to your child about this, and everything.

This same questioning technique should be applied to the child's school situation. Ask the youngster how he's doing in all of his classes; how he feels about all of his teachers. In evaluating the tutoring process, also, of course, stay in touch with the tutor, i.e., talk to the tutor as well, monitoring pupil progress from the tutor's viewpoint, as well as your child's. Discuss with the tutor his philosophies of instruction and pertinent attitudes that he might bring to this very important process. On an ongoing basis, discuss with him the plans and strategies that he has in mind for your child. He (or she) is the expert and you should not be telling her how to "run the show." However, you should ask questions, keep "in the game," and make suggestions if you want to.

Let the tutor know that you want to be involved and would desire suggestions on how you might be able to help your child during the time when she is not seeing you. In other words, how can you help out with homework and/or assignments - both those in school and those given to your child by the tutor? In addition, request assignments and other practice work for your child, if, of course, the tutor agrees. Thus, the pupil can derive maximum and ongoing benefit and "mileage" from a single given lesson. Through this varied combination of "checks," the parent can effectively monitor the tutoring program. Again, much of this discussion is useful in hiring any tutor, not one specializing simply in SAT/ACT.

Chapter Thirteen

Student Views

At this point I will again present some of the thoughts that have arisen from the musings of several of my current (and past) high school students. We will hear from some tenth graders as they approach the critical eleventh grade. Among these pupils that I highlight (as well as thousands of others) there are many different ideas regarding the SAT/ACT and the entire process. Some know next to nothing about the process while others (though certainly not the majority) know quite a bit. And of course there's a lot of "in between" knowledge and insight. Some have lots of anxiety - some not much at all. There certainly are quite a large number of misconceptions regarding 11th grade and all these exams. We will also hear from eleventh graders.

It is quite obvious that pupils need to be better educated regarding the process they are about to enter. The myths need to be dispelled. Pupils need "road maps," guidelines, guidance, support, and very importantly, knowledge about the upcoming process and how to best approach it and deal with it. Knowledge truly is "power." And this power will translate into confidence, points on exams and the relief of much of the unnecessary stress that plagues many pupils. Again, all this is another important reason for pupils and parents to read this entire book.

We will then hear from some twelfth graders - veterans of the whole process. These pupils look back on that frenzied time and relate their feelings of relief after the fact. They thus can provide guidance, support and insight for those "rookies" to the entire situation. Let us hear from "Susan," an 11th grader:

In casual conversation with people, I am at times asked what grade I'm going into and with my response comes a rush of laughter, pity, and advice. "Junior year," I say, and all at once I am no longer a fun, likeable, sweet girl, but someone who is facing the mind and innocence - destroying corruption of standardized testing.

SATs, ACTs, and SAT II's seem to be the primary cause for all these reactions. We, the victims of these conversations, flail our hands in the air and run screaming in the opposite direction. Everyone I talk to says the exact same thing: "junior year is really rough." Yet I don't really see the big deal with these so called "life-ruining" tests. Maybe it is because I come from an area of the country where AP classes and end - of - the - course AP tests are more prevalent and more frightening among students; thus, compared to these AP's, standardized testing seems like a breeze, with of course, the right preparation. So when I hear the words, "SAT or ACT," I don't have to be carried away on a stretcher, because, to me, there are things much worse and harder than standardized testing.

SAT - type tests do not seem that nerve racking to me. You study so far in advance and are permitted to take the test more than once. Thus, it's not as if blowing it the first time will "mess up" your life. As mentioned, these tests, when compared to others, such as AP tests, do not seem so extremely challenging and are, from what I've heard from peers, somewhat bearable. The media seems to make this test seem impossible and torturous but, I think, in reality, the SAT and PSAT are just more annoying tests, like the HSPA (NJ "exit" exam), that juniors are required to take. Also, a lot of these tests seem to be based more on trickery than on testing intelligence. From what I've heard, you have to know and understand how the writer of the test thinks and this with some added talent in the intellectual world will surely lead to success. To understand the chaotic minds of the writers, a tutor or class is required. As long as the right preparation is put in, there's no reason why we shouldn't do fine.

There's a lot about the ACT that I don't really understand, but from what I've heard, it's more math oriented (and science?). I think the ACT is a more straightforward test, unlike the SAT, which involves unnecessary trickery. In my opinion, the ACT is more worthwhile because doing well on it, to me, truly proves intelligence, rather than succeeding on an SAT, where studying the material will not necessarily lead to a satisfying score. I'm pretty sure that now, nearly all colleges accept ACT scores from students who do better on the ACT than on the SAT, so I would say take both, but I think the ACT is a much better test overall.

The tests that are more challenging, in my opinion, are the ones that are focused on one subject area. These tests are the SAT Twos and the AP end-of-course tests and they are the ones to worry about. AP tests address information from the entire course, making three weeks of intense studying barely enough. They usually consist of multiple choice, short answers, free response, and at least one essay. I'm pretty sure that for this test, there are no secrets or trickery; it's all intelligence. And you only get one chance. If you fail, you do not get credit for the course towards college, which was the reason of putting yourself through the torture from the beginning. So, pretty much, if you fail, it was all for nothing. SAT Twos are not as difficult as AP tests, but still require the strong knowledge of a subject. These tests are an hour long and (I think) all multiple choice, so when compared to the AP test, they are a breeze. However, they are harder than normal SATs because of the condensed knowledge required. SAT Twos seem to me to be kind of like a final exam in a given subject. If you take an AP test, you should definitely take the SAT II test for that subject because it will be extremely easy and will look good on a college application if you do extremely well. If you don't take an AP test, you could still take one or more SAT Twos, but they will probably require the amount of studying that students take going into an AP test and you might have to learn some more information than taught to you in your normal course.

Ok, so I was wrong; junior year is rough. With all the standardized testing and not to mention, harder class work, it will undoubtedly be tough, especially if you choose to take any AP classes. However, it is not as bad as people make it out to be. Yes, there is a lot of extra work, alongside class work, that must be put in, but year after year, people get through it and survive, so I know that I, and all of the other future juniors, can too.

Let us look at the musings of the student who wrote the essay just presented - we called her "Susan." Although she is not really an "average" "rising" junior, her essay does contain some very interesting points for us to discuss. She's not "typical" since she seems to have taken or will be taking a large number of AP courses. She also attends school at a very competitive district where pupils often start talking about SAT's not long after they learn their ABC's. So she would likely be placed in the "above the average knowledge about eleventh grade" category. However, her comments still warrant discussion.

She does not seem as concerned about SAT/ACT testing as she is about the even more rigorous AP testing. She does have some basis here to justify the lower degree of her anxieties. She has spoken to her friends who've been through the SAT/ACT process and have reassured her that it's truly not "that" bad. Many pupils do not have this view - and have much larger anxieties.

In New Jersey the High School "exit" exam is the HSPA. Most states have similar exams. Depending on your state the exit exams are generally not nearly as rigorous as the SAT or ACT and most states "curve" those exit exams so most pupils eventually succeed.

Sue has heard that the SAT is a "tricky" test and she is correct. It seems that the SAT has become known as "tricky" while the ACT is more "straightforward." For example, Sue had heard that if she knew, say, the formula for the area of a circle then on the ACT she might only need to "plug in numbers" on many problems; however, on the SAT, relatively simple material is embedded in at times outrageously "tricky" questions. The SAT is more for "critical" thinkers. Sue knows that pupils should always take both ACT and SAT. It is amazing how many pupils (here in 2012 - 2013, especially in the Northeast) know next to nothing about the ACT.

Sue believes that the ACT is "more worthwhile" and "proves intelligence." Once again both tests have their respective assets and liabilities and each test may favor one pupil over another. Take both!

Sue says that the SAT II and APs are the exams to "worry about." Truly, there shouldn't be "severe worry," just a normal amount of "healthy apprehension." She thinks that failure on an AP renders the course "all for nothing." One should come out of all these exams with knowledge that one did one's best (assuming preparation was adequate) and one will use the examination experience as a "learning curve" that will not only enhance future scores but will help the pupil in his overall educational process.

Sue knows a lot more about the "SAT Twos" than most "rising" juniors. She knows that if you take an AP class, say AP Biology, then it might very well be a good idea to take the Biology SAT II, optimally, in fact, during the same year that you take the AP course.

Best of all, Sue seems to have kept a lot in perspective. She realizes that she, like millions who came before her, will survive her junior year quite nicely!

Next we hear from a "gifted" senior who has been through it all:

It's hard to find a high school student for whom the thought of standardized testing doesn't evoke a strong emotional response. For many, the letters S-A-T cause as much fear, stress, and anxiety as Chris Griffin's evil monkey in the closet. Others have mastered this test, and can reflect on their excellent score to gain confidence. Still others feel confused and lost, surrounded by countless deadlines and forms, dealing simultaneously with counselors, the College Board and admissions officers, not even knowing where to begin. What is common in all cases, however, is that a standardized test has come to be seen as one of the biggest milestones in a high school student's career.

Why? From a rational point of view, after all, this is simply a long but simple test. The math section requires no advanced knowledge of trigonometry or calculus. The writing section tests grammar rules which have been reinforced time after time, from middle school forward. The reading section is a test of just that, reading and understanding, something which we can all do. As for the college process, admissions deans constantly insist that the SAT will neither make nor break a candidate. Its small role in the process is diminishing further, as some schools no longer even ask for your scores.

Yet despite these facts, anxiety about this test has never been higher. People hire expensive private tutors in all different areas in the hope of boosting their scores. Businesses such as Kaplan and the Princeton Review, which offer courses and sell prep books, are thriving. It is common for students to take the test three or more times, combining their top scores from each section to create the best possible profile of themselves.

If you are worried about the SAT - and the odds are that if you're reading this book, then you are - then let me begin what I have to say to you with this:

Stop. Calm down, and take a deep breath. It's all going to be okay.

Keep in mind; this isn't coming from some far-off admissions counselor who you suspect may be trying to trick you. My name is Jim, a recent high school graduate who has lived through the most recent college admissions cycle. I'm not talking about the way colleges were back when your parents went to school; I'm talking about the way they are now. And unless your parents have made an active effort to stay current with college admissions trends, their own experiences in this one specific area probably won't be of all that much help.

The fact is this: the SATs are not what they used to be. If you're not good enough to get into Harvard, then a 2400 isn't going to help you. Conversely, if you've done everything you can and have a solid shot at getting in, a poor performance on the SAT won't stop you. In almost all cases, a person's SAT scores merely offer confirmation as to what a college has already figured out about a person.

The anxiety begins when people wonder what will happen if their SAT score does not accurately reflect their ability. An admissions officer reviewing an application now has two conflicting sets of information. On the one hand, a person's transcript, recommendations, extracurriculars, and other records paint one portrait of the person. On the other hand, the SAT says that this candidate is not as qualified as the first set of information would suggest.

What happens now? To answer that, I suggest you put yourself in this person's position. You know that the first set of information has been compiled over the course of many, many years. Recommendations come from a careful analysis of the candidate's academic achievements and character qualities. That grade on a transcript comes from a full year of hard work. The SAT, on the other hand, is a 4 hour test taken on a groggy Saturday morning. One missed bubble, dropped negative, or similar boredom-induced careless error could cost upwards of 30 or 40 points. Clearly, the first set of information is much more reliable. Remember this: when information from the SAT conflicts other sources, the other sources are dominant.

You are probably thinking right now that I have not helped you improve your score in any way. But why would I? There are professionals who do that. I could tell you that the essay doesn't leave enough room to write five decent paragraphs, so better to stick to four. I could tell you that if a math problem leaves you stuck with a senseless jumble of variables, you can plug in sensible numbers for the variables and work from there. I could tell you that if there is no direct evidence for an answer in a reading passage, it is almost definitely not the answer. But I'm not just going to give you random tips like that. The fact is that for every question I have seen and every trick I have learned, there are 10 other questions or tricks out there that I don't know. If you've already decided that you want to get some sort of professional SAT prep - and again, if you're reading this book, you probably have - then I'm certainly not going to stop you. In fact, it's probably a good idea - I myself had many hours of tutoring. These people will help you will learn your strengths, pinpoint your weaknesses, and be far more helpful than even the best quick tips on a page.

But perhaps I can help you create the right mental approach to the SATs. I truly believe that the vast majority of the stress surrounding the SATs is caused by the belief that they are important and stress - worthy. Of course, this mindset is a sort of self-fulfilling prophecy.

Don't buy it.

I'm not saying that you shouldn't study for the SATs. Go to a tutor, learn your vocabulary, practice your math, and do your absolute best . . . but not at the expense of your sanity. I promise you, there is a middle ground, and the people who strike that balance will get the most return for their efforts. You can't succeed if you're constantly stressed out, wondering how many math errors will cost you that letter of admission from Princeton, how many more will cost you Emory, and how many will cost you getting in anywhere it all.

The SATs are annoying, and there isn't any way around that fact. But if you view it not as a life - changing experience, but rather as a minor nuisance which you just need to do your best on and then keep moving, you will find the process significantly easier and more bearable. And hey, you might just find yourself a little time to go out during your junior year.

Here is the view of "Marty," another "gifted" senior who relates his views on the SAT process:

Taking the SAT? This might interest you. As a senior, it's pretty clear to me in hindsight that the SAT test and its corollary subject tests were completely manageable. There's always preparation to be done, but that shouldn't be surprising or phasing after years of school. So many people, too many in fact, reach the point where the stress to do well on these, frankly, basic tests begins to outweigh the level of importance of the actual test. People can even psych themselves out on the day of the test, and underperform. The trick is to remember that the SAT is just a test. Odds are that your Precalculus or British Literature grade will have more of a bearing on your college future than this SAT score.

It is also worth saying that it is not a competitive test. Do not feel obliged to tell your friends what you got (although you may want to, which is fine), nor guilty about retaking it. Sometimes the magic works, sometimes it doesn't. Someone will get a 2250 or a 2400. If it is you, congratulations on your immense success. If, as I assume is the case, that someone is not you, be proud of what you did get, and don't compare yourself to them. You aren't them. You will only end up feeling bad about a perfectly fine score. I've seen hordes of people in my school do this, and it's never pretty.

Don't forget, too, that this is not the be-all and end-all of tests. Once again, this will not determine your future, despite the common consensus. Proper preparation and a good common sense will get you through it. Do remember, though, that the SAT is a VERY long test. It is upwards of 4 hours, early in the morning, and you might find yourself in a different school, among total strangers. Don't let this bother you. Some of my best scores were in other schools. You're there to take the test, and anything outside of that is secondary. Remember that if you're having a hard time acclimating to the test center.

Be sure to go to sleep at a time that will give you at the minimum 8 hours of rest. Wake up early enough to eat a solid, balanced breakfast, and don't leave with barely enough time to get there. If it's hot, dress lightly (sandals are fine), and if it's cold, wear layers. It's better to take off a jacket and have a sweatshirt still on than to be cold after taking off your sole heavy coat. Get to your testing center early enough that you can get a bit lost if it isn't your regular school. Make sure the night before you have all of the supplies you need, and don't be afraid to bring more than you need, identification-wise. Finally, on another note, don't make plans afterwards. I say this because as you step out of the nearly 5 hour exam, you will almost certainly want nothing to do besides nap. I know I did, and so did all of my friends.

Don't stack up too many subject tests on the same day, and follow all the same rules above when preparing for them. Talk to your teachers about them too, as they can be your best friends for studying subject material. And, if you find that you honestly and truly aren't prepared to take the test, reschedule it to a later month. I did for the SAT Two Math exam, and I think it was the right choice.

Definitely spend at least a month lightly studying, which I take for granted you are already doing. While cramming isn't something that works alone for studying, doing some the week before, on top of the months of regular prep, can help too, provided you don't burn yourself out. Also, avoid studying on the night before the exam, for the same reason. Most of all, don't worry too hard about it. You got this. Trust me: I'm a senior.

Now we hear from "Barbara," a fairly "average" senior:

I took the SAT's twice: once in eleventh grade and once in the twelfth. The reason that I took it again in the 12th grade is that the first time I didn't understand how to take the SAT. The SAT isn't a hard test. The reason I suggest that test takers should study very hard for the SAT is because there is a strategy that should be mastered in order to pass. You have to understand how to answer the questions. The first time I took the SAT, I felt like it was in a language I didn't understand.

Barbara is typical of certain twelfth graders who are about to graduate from high school. Barbara took the SAT in eleventh grade. She is a pretty decent student but for some reason did not prepare much for the SAT in her junior year. Not knowing much about the exam, she allowed it to overwhelm her. She received a low score and as she implied, she felt as if it were in a foreign language.

With the rude awakening (a resounding wake up call), she, as many like her, got serious over the summer, buckled down, learned all about the exam, practiced profusely and did fairly well in Grade 12. Her advice is basically not to procrastinate, do what you need to do, learn about the exam and how to prepare for it and go to it! She, like most, are going to college and feel that the exam should not be the roadblock that many make it out to be.

We now hear from a variety of tenth graders - pupils who are set to get into the whole SAT/ACT exam "game." Again some of these kids know very little, if anything at all, about the exam. Some know a bit. And others, they know a significant amount about it.

Ernie and Tommy give us a little insight into the minds of the "rising" junior (those just about set to begin 11th grade):

Ernie: As of now I am a tenth grader entering the eleventh grade. In my junior year I will take the SAT's. In my opinion it does not really seem different from any other tests except it is a lot more important. A lot of people are usually worried about the test but I think it's better not to worry because it sometimes causes you to black out and lose focus. Personally I'm not worried about the test as far as panicking. Overall it is an important test because it depends on your college. A good way to study is to take SAT practice tests so you know what to expect.

Tommy: As of now I am in the tenth grade moving up to the eleventh grade. My math teacher Mr. Richman asked me about the SAT. Honestly I don't know anything about the SAT, but when I take it I can honestly say that I will be nervous. I think it is very important in college. I think it considers where you stand. Now to study I would go to the library and just use an SAT book to study or use the internet. Just do what I can to pass.

The brief pieces from Tom and Ernie seem more typical of an "average" (or below average) rising junior. Ernie doesn't really seem to know too much about the upcoming exams but he does seem to have his anxiety level under control. He certainly is not a "gifted" pupil but with an education about the exams and a study plan, he should maximize his potential.

Tommy admits that he honestly knows nothing about the exam except that it will be important for college. He says he will be nervous and has a vague study plan.

So we see there is a wide variation in the amounts of knowledge our high school pupils possess with regard to the SAT/ACT Examination process.

As far as Will and Marty were concerned, they presented the thoughts and reflections of highly gifted students. For the majority, these feelings are not shared. For the average and "below average" pupil, there usually is more anxiety and struggle. It would be great if all could feel as confident as Will.

Tommy and Ernie represent the pupil on the other end of the spectrum. They are not consumed by gaining admission to the Ivy League. They are hard working and often academically challenged, yet hard work, exam prep, and knowledge of exam logistics will also carry them to college success. Success is for all!

Chapter Fourteen

Make Room for the Kid

This chapter is appropriate for students and/or parents. Most participants in the "study game" often do not think about the "turf" on which this study takes place. In sports we see that many teams do better "at home" rather than "away." They feel more comfortable. This is one reason why it is important to register early for your SAT and ACT exams: you will get to take the exam at the location of your choice - usually your hometown high school - where you will be the home team and likely will perform better than you would at a "strange" site.

Pupils should decide where it is that they would like to do most of their studying. Parents who read this will gain insight into these important "affective" factors that will enhance exam results by helping to guide their children into environments where study will be maximized. That is the purpose of this brief chapter. In my years as a staff developer and also in the years as a teacher, I came to understand the importance of study environment. Hence, "Make Room for the Kid."

So again, study environment is of great importance and its consideration will aid in exam outcome and translate down the road into great numbers of points!

For socializing, oftentimes people choose a restaurant because of its "atmosphere" - it is quiet and conducive to talking, listening, relating, relaxing, and enjoying. At other times, folks seek a "party-animal" atmosphere replete with noise, music, excitement. Well, for studying and learning, the key really is that it must be just right for learning - it should be well-lit, quiet and comfortable, supplied with appropriate desk, chair and atmosphere. Your child's room, in other words, must be totally set up for academic success. Walk through the room and check it out from ceiling to floor and from every corner.

Tailor it to suit the needs of your child - an effectively set up and well-prepared room will make studying and learning that much easier. Keep in mind, however, that often, pupils need variety in their study environments. For example, for me, growing up and studying for years and years (I even attended medical school for a little over two years), I usually required a variety of ever-changing atmospheres to study most efficiently. At times I thrived in the total quiet and solitude of my "room." However, at other times, I worked most efficiently on: a) the beach, b) the bus or train, or c) long plane rides. At times, I wanted to study in the library (where I could take "socialization" breaks). At yet other times, however, I preferred a restaurant or even the local Barnes and Noble cafe. The pupil in question needs to experiment in all kinds of different atmospheres before he zeros in on what will be most appropriate for him at a given point.

In other words, all pupils, since they must spend so much time in study mode, often need to vary the scenery and experiment to discover methods of achieving maximum functioning. So, even a factor that seems as minor as study environment can truly be major.

There are children who, unfortunately, may not have a great variety of home study choices - their rooms might be tiny, non-existent, extremely noisy or shared by any number of siblings. Here is where the child must branch out to those other venues - libraries, schools, bookstores, friend's homes, etc. In some H.S. Calculus classes, students have even been known to participate in "Calculus Study Parties," among other creatively wonderful ideas. What about music? Or TV? Again these questions can be answered only by pupil trial and error. Some can work effectively with music, but TV, for most, is just too distracting. Study environment is quite important to your SAT/ACT success!

Chapter Fifteen

Parents Can Help Out:
The Circle of (Parenting) Success

This Chapter will hopefully assist you in developing an overall philosophy and "procedure" in dealing with issues related to your child and school (and even more!).

The "Circle of Life" is a song in "Lion King." In Chapter 11, we have the "Circle of (SAT/ACT) Success." In the center of the graphic is "Very Successful SAT/ACT Results." This can be effected via a combination of all ingredients "orbiting" this central "sun." There are other circles for other situations. For example, there is a Circle of Effective Classroom Teaching from a teacher's point of view. It is a reflection of the theme of my teacher's manual, "Just Let Me Survive Today." There is the Circle of Success for the camp counselor, reflecting the ideas contained in my book "The Ultimate Camp Counselor Manual."

For the parent, in the Appendix we have the "orbiting" Circle of (Parental) Success. Each component in the circle has been (or will be) mentioned in this book and makes up a huge aspect of what is needed for successful parenting, at least with respect to school. And, of course, many of these attitudes and practices, when applied, will result not only in a successful and happy student, but also in a successful and happy "kid", not only in school, but also during his or her entire life. So let's recap some of the critical "Circle of (Parental) Success (Appendix Figure 4)."

First, let's examine "Positive Reinforcement." This involves responding to the success (and near success, and even failures) and efforts of your child. Be aware of them, ask about them - be sure your child knows that you care. Be a cheerleader, an encourager. Make your child feel good. This will help to strengthen that all-important kid self-esteem. Praise, praise, praise. And then encourage, recognize, reward, discuss, motivate . . . notice!

A closely related input here is "Communication." Talk to your child. Be honest with her. Let her know you're there for her to discuss questions, problems, homework, anything. No question is too minor or insignificant or "stupid." Incidentally, eliminate the word "stupid" from all family vocabularies. It is hurtful and damaging! Encourage the feeling in your child that he can be free to ask ANYTHING at ANYTIME! Talk over dinner, in the car, on the bus. Communicate. Listen. Spend that "Quality Time" with your child, 'cause if you don't, forget about communication.

Listen to Harry Chapin's "Cat's in the Cradle." If you don't have time for your children, they will quickly turn off to you and seek to communicate and spend time elsewhere - with friends, with the TV, the world of fantasy, the Internet, the "bad crowd," the gang - with who knows who, or what. You will be well on your way to losing control and sadly wondering what happened, when (perhaps) years later (or perhaps only months later) you'll be sitting at that suspension hearing or in that police precinct begging for a second chance. Communicate and Spend Time. Just Do It!

You must develop a "Philosophy of Parenting" which will form the central theme around which you will conduct your entire parental business. Mine? I seek to treat my child with utmost respect and kindness. I seek to always try to build her self-esteem and confidence. I have a set of behavioral rules which I try to firmly, yet lovingly, enforce. I try to teach values, and the importance of getting along with and treating others with kindness and respect. Values include, but are not limited to: teamwork, sportsmanship, caring, integrity, and courage. I seek to inject a positive and hopeful attitude with the desire, if needed, to seek the assistance and help of trusted friends, family, and trained professionals when indicated.

As an Assistant Principal, I was required to develop a Philosophy of Education. I reprint it in Figure 2 (the Appendix) because it will become truly meaningful in the context of this discussion.

Your philosophy of successful parenting should influence the methods you use, not only in the educational situation, but in all areas of your parenting techniques. The remaining components of my circle are actually further results of my philosophy of parenting.

"Sense of Humor" is self-explanatory. One should always try to cultivate a sense of humor. Often it helps defuse potentially serious confrontational situations. Just as an example, you might be trying to put your two year old daughter's pajamas on and be met with serious resistance, a la kicking and screaming. You quickly would introduce "Cookie Monster" or "Big Bird" creatively into the situation, and magically, laughter replaces agony - and the bedtime ritual becomes a pleasure.

Chapters in my teaching manual are devoted to situations where humor has been highly successful in defusing potentially disastrous confrontational classroom possibilities. Of course this is not always advisable or easy. Use your judgment. However, it is true that for these situations, as well as other parenting issues - our next component is heavily involved - that of "Patience and Perseverance." The effective teacher, the effective parent, needs to possess these - big time.

It is a simple given - that oftentimes our kids need for us to try, as far as possible, to be patient - in most areas. Be patient with their behaviors and patient with their personal and educational progress. As a tutor, I have parents actually expecting dramatic and almost immediate results: reading scores going from 3rd grade to 6th in a week, or math averages skyrocketing to 90 from 70 within a month. There's got to be an understanding that (true) change often requires (lots of) time. Sometimes it can occur quickly, but most times it is slow and difficult. If your child is under the guidance of good people* (teachers, tutors, enlightened parents, therapists, friends, relatives, or whoever may be necessary) and has achieved a true <u>desire</u> to change (via help from some of these same people or just by a maturation process involving self-growth) patience will still be an absolute requirement. And the more patient all are, the quicker the results will come. Of course, there may be a time will arrive when a slight "push" might be indicated. You consult with your good people (see * above) and make your "push" decision.

Perseverance is the "next door neighbor" of patience. Because this patience is going to require perseverance. There will inevitably be pressures. There may be relapses - but try to see to it that (large and small) setbacks will not deter you in your progress toward success. You cannot quit - cannot let your child quit. You must all be strong and must "hang tough." This tenacity often makes the difference between the winners and losers in this "Circle Game" of life.

We then, of course, have the "wise old" component - "Experience." It is the great teacher. As we get through our various issues, we get better and better at knowing how to handle problems in the future. The quest will not be quite as difficult. Here also is where we can call on the experiences of other trusted people who might, just by relating knowledge and advice to us (via conversation or action) ease our burden and lessen our degree of stress enormously. This leads us to "Networking" as the next important component in our Circle.

First, however, let's look at "Self-Education" for parents. There are many pieces involved in this component. Parents should want to learn more about their children's studies.

For example, they may want to be able to help their kids with algebra, but either had not studied it for years or perhaps had never studied it at all. These parents should be encouraged to take courses in this subject area or in any other area they might be interested in. This way, they might actually be able to sit down with their child and render some assistance with the material. Of course, even if they are or become "subject area smart," there is still much to know about the instructional process that results in successful learning. However, at least the parent is showing signs of great interest to the pupil.

Besides subject area self-education, parents should also become as familiar as possible with those parenting techniques that would be helpful here, learning everything they can about issues that children of the particular age group in question must face: coping strategies, motivational methods and other pertinent pointers. In other words, the pursuit of self-education in every way possible can only result in positive outcomes.

The more a parent learns about parenting strategies from the experts the better his child is going to do both academically and emotionally. In our "Circle of Success," we see that parents who are willing to become learners will first improve their knowledge of subject matter and parenting skills, and second they are setting an example for their children of someone who values education and sees the great benefits that it can generate. The Circle Component of Self-Education thus has deep meaning, far beyond that which is at first evident.

We also will note the linkages of several Circle Components. First we reiterate the notion of "Street Smarts." In our discussions we have made frequent reference to the fact that quite often, parents are in the "dark" about the status of their children - both emotionally and academically. The "wool" has often been pulled over their eyes. Well, it is time for them to WAKE UP!

Through self-education and increased self-awareness, the empowered parent is no longer the pushover. This in itself will serve as role model material for the shocked pupil. "My parent has woken up and I no longer am in charge here. She has made positive change in her life - she's taken control here - and - I like it."

If you go to an ATM machine at 3 AM, would you walk in and out oblivious to the possible dangers? Would you even go there at all? No - because you are "street-smart," aware, shrewd, smart, sharp, intelligent, alert, mature, cautious, responsible. Act the same way in all aspects of your child's functioning. Take charge, be an aware, responsible parent - know what's going on - be "Street Smart."

When you take charge in this way, you're awareness will point you toward the essentials of "Notebook Monitoring." You will ask your child to show you his notebook and you will know exactly what to look for. In fact, you will not stop at notebook monitoring - you will check out report cards, texts, tests, etc. You'll be openly communicating with your child. As far as that notebook however, you will be examining it in detail with an eye toward "Early Detection" of problems. That notebook will tell you what it is your child is learning day by day; it will give you views into his attention, attendance and concentration. As with cancer, the key to preventing malignant school problems is "Early Detection" (another circle component), which can be accomplished by notebook monitoring as well as by communicating and spending that quality time. All the ingredients are beginning to coalesce and intertwine.

Now how can we better see to it that this early detection and effective monitoring take place? Well, we've already spoken about the notions of street smarts and self-education. Let's discuss a few other ideas.

One is seen in the Circle Component of "Networking With the Entire School Community." We hit on this earlier in the book. There are oh so many people in the school community who can and are supremely willing to help out: there are the teachers, administrators, team of social work professionals and all the other support staff at the school. And this small army will be able to refer you to even more sources of assistance. By networking with this vast community of people, you will gain enormous insight into the learning process and into sources of assistance for your child. Gradually, the probability for success for your child is increasing dramatically.

If necessary, "Referrals" will be made. We will report what had been said previously. In other words, assuming that there is going to be a need for other than the usual methods of assistance, channels have been set up (throughout this book) for you to obtain a "referral" to the appropriate expert - be it a math or science tutor, a special education evaluation, a speech therapist, a psychologist, social worker, psychiatrist, general practitioner, dentist, lawyer, or whoever. As in Chapter 11, the Circle of Success is almost complete. Soon, its pieces will magically link together and begin spinning. Lights will shine, bells will sound, and whistles will be heard. It soon will be time to celebrate and rejoice! Notice the aforementioned "melting together" of the various inputs from our Circle.

While all these other pieces are as simmering components of a "Success Stew," there are yet other processes at work. One is "PTA Participation." In other words, the parent advocate must join and become an active member of the school PTA. He must attend meetings, do volunteer work and even become an officer of the Association. Why is this membership so significant? Number one, it is a further way of networking - with teachers, fellow-parents who have similar concerns, administrators and even pupils. As a member of the group you will have the opportunity for enlisting informative speakers for PTA meetings, which will be of direct benefit to all parents in attendance.

In addition, parents often can wield considerable power in many areas of school functioning. They are regularly mandated (assistant) members of committees often charged with helping make school policy, writing, creating and/or recommending curricula, formulating budgets, and hiring, firing and evaluating teachers and administrators. The benefits of being active members of your school PTA's (or PTO's) are enormous and this makes up another valuable component of the "Circle of Success."

We have discussed at length the notion of "Discipline With Dignity." We saw that no matter what, our children must be treated with respect and all dealings must be aimed at maintaining their self - images at a healthy level. We won't go into the details again. However, it appears in the Circle because without its inclusion, there can be no success stories written: the Circle will just fall apart into pieces - it can be looked upon as glue that holds this oftentimes fragile Circle together. It is necessary!

We include "Study Techniques" in our Circle. There are many pupils out there who reach the state of readiness for learning but lack proper guidance in the procedures or actual techniques of studying. They simply do not know how to do it. It can be extremely frustrating for them. They need to receive instruction here. Where will they get it? From teachers, from "how to study" classes, from trial and error. Also, of exceptional help here is the one on one tutoring that can be provided by experts in this area. Perhaps your guidance counselor can help out too. In any event, one of the most important ingredients in classroom success is for pupils to be "street smart" on study strategies. It is an absolute necessity. Enormous is the number of pupils who simply do not know how to study and prepare for exams, how to become organized, how to write term papers, how to know how to do - whatever. With your valuable guidance, your child will eventually (as quickly as possible) learn study techniques and good habits in these areas.

As you become a better, more informed, in touch, "street smart" parent yourself, you will become intimately more familiar with the needs of your child - from every point of view. This will allow you to conduct an informal "Needs Assessment" for your child. In other words, you will become more adept at attempting to diagnose the problems of your children and in being able to quickly act on ameliorating them via all of the components of our "Circle of Success." So, "Needs Assessment" becomes one of the initial pieces in the successful story that we are composing here.

"Do The Right Thing" is a Circle Component that really is synonymous with values education. We touched on this before when we were talking about our philosophies. We always strive to have our kids think about doing the right thing - i.e., treating others with caring and respect and always living by standards of high integrity, courage, teamwork and honesty. Doing the right thing, again, can serve as the national anthem of the successful pupil and person. So there we have it, the culminating chapter of our book - the summary of what it's all about.

Study that (Parental) Circle of Success. The more familiar you become with it and its significance, the closer you will be to arriving at its central theme - student success. Because it is of such critical importance, let us <u>briefly</u> summarize and organize.

First, you form a philosophy of parenting. Hopefully, it contains much of what we've been advocating here. You establish rapport with your child through open communication and spending quality time with him. Via self-education, PTA involvement and networking with the entire school community you begin to acquire street smarts about your child and his behaviors, attitudes and practices. Via your communications with him and your inspections of his notebook and other work outputs (including examination of exams and tests), you will become quite able to detect and act on (early and via referral if necessary) potential problems. At times your child may not be so open to sharing with you his notebook, exam results, quizzes, etc. At times you may not be able to get much information about his "Day." So . . . you try . . . you do your best . . . you let him know that you're there and you're interested. Be interested! Hopefully you've established good practice early on.

Also, at different points in your child's education, he may be more or less receptive to your involvement. Play it by ear but keep your "street smarts" antennae always on "open."

Your positive reinforcement will help build self - esteem in your son. You will deal discipline with dignity so self - respect will be maintained, and positive behaviors will result. Your child will know to "Do the Right Thing." Your patience, perseverance and experience, touched with your sense of humor will help greatly in character development in your child and yourself. Your inculcation of healthy values will further help mold character and self-respect in your offspring.

Your skill as a burgeoning diagnostician will help you to compose a detailed and effective needs assessment. You will also help your child with his study techniques (or in helping her discover it) which will help her to succeed big time in her studies. When difficulties do rear their ugly heads (and they usually do), you will be able to not only help your child to cope with them but will also be able to recognize the need to seek experts when problems reach a certain threshold. Yes, this "Circle of Success" is of critical significance.

Recently I attended a lecture by a well - known child psychologist. He had written a book which I bought at the lecture. My daughter was in grade seven and was approaching her "adolescent, volatile, teen years." She was beginning to exhibit all sorts of changes - behavioral, attitudinal, etc. The lecture and book were great and I recommend them to help you understand "adolescence" and all of its issues. What is important here to me is that I thought some of the issues I was having were "abnormal" and not shared by most other parents. Yet most of them would shake their heads in knowing agreement - yes, they shared some of the same problems. I thought it was only me who had these issues and feelings. No you're one of millions.

Your child is unique. Teaching and tutoring certainly brought this out . . . every pupil has some issue, some problem, something to deal with. Your Circle of Success is certainly unique for you. It's your circle. It has the same components as other kids but each component functions differently for each different child. Welcome to the club!

Chapter Sixteen

That's A Wrap: Putting It All Together

I hope you enjoyed reading my manual. More importantly, parents and pupils, I hope you derived from it some valuable information and insights into achieving success on the SAT and/or ACT exams. This is an important time period in your life and I have tried to help ease your journey. In fact, hopefully, it might even turn into an enjoyable challenge and allow you to cherish this entire high school experience. Don't let test prep "rattle" you. Stay cool and keep it in its proper perspective.

To further summarize my message, we once again refer to the SAT/ACT "Circle of Success" found in the Appendix and earlier in the book.

As you begin your SAT/ACT prep process, you will try to assess your ability at your "starting point." You will use your PSAT/Kaplan/Princeton Review tests to establish this baseline status. This early detection will help you to discern your needs. You will then decide what method of test prep to use: group, one on one, or solo. You will then "network with the world" in order to help you select the proper texts and support materials, test logistics and actual exam content.

You will consult with your parents, friends, teachers and relatives to help guide you. Collegeboard.com and ACTstudent.org will offer even more support in your quest to maximize your exam potential. Your self-education process continues as you also begin and/or continue your college networking procedures. Your exam prep involves the hard work reflected by your practice,

practice, practice sessions. And as in most major endeavors, you will be patient, you will persevere and you will always learn from your experience.

We've discussed the types of books you should purchase to help guide you; what kind of tutoring to search for and how to determine which type is best for you; the logistics of taking the exams, i.e., matters of timing, guessing, strategies; the various musings of children involved with the exam - from seniors who've taken it to sophomores and juniors who are in various stages of preparation; what goes into a great essay and how to achieve success with it; the specific details of preparation for math, reading, vocabulary, writing, grammar, and science; the difference between the SAT and ACT and how to capitalize on these differences; and psychological adjustments you should make as well as positive thoughts you should focus on. Finally, we have shown you that all students can most absolutely improve their test performance and achieve their maximum potential - and beyond!

The ingredients in the "Circle of Success" when combined and nurtured, will result in enhanced (perhaps much enhanced) test performance. Enjoy your high school years, take these exams (another "rite of passage" of adolescence) in stride, work hard, hang in there, and I'm sure this wonderful period in your life will be happy, challenging, and very very rewarding and successful!

I hope that this book has been of great help to you. Again, I hope you enjoyed reading it as much as I enjoyed writing it. I have been tutoring SAT/ACT for many, many years now. It is truly very rewarding for me to see pupils improve their SAT/ACT scores. And as we've seen, their improvement can most surely take place. However, it does not occur without hard work and insight on the part of the pupil. By writing this guide, I hoped to supply some of the insights that you will require. Much of the hard work, of course, is up to you!

Appendix

FIGURE ONE
WHO AM I?

To appreciate the spirit of this manual, I believe it is extremely important to know about the author. Understanding how my professional career developed will be a great step toward feeling the force behind the ideas inherent in this manual.

I was a camper in a summer "sleep-away" camp beginning in 1959. It was known (and still is in 2012) as "Trail's End Camp." The mottos of the camp were "Truth, Ethics, Courage," and "Better for Having Been at Trail's End Camp." I later went on to become a counselor, group leader, assistant athletic director and "Director of Mishigos" - Yiddish for craziness. Over and over the mottos were reinforced by conferences, seminars and day to day camp life. I also realized the importance of having fun and "acting silly" from time to time. Armed with 24 years of camping experience and no student teaching, I became a New York City junior high school math teacher.

That first year was "trial by fire." Everything was extremely difficult. The pupils were so hard to control. I was required to take a "beginning teacher's course" and there I would go each week and commiserate with all the other new teachers. However, I learned a lot from this course. I received pointers and suggestions from my enthusiastic and sympathetic colleagues and from the veteran mentors who knew how things should be done. And you high school people think that ninth graders are babies? Teach in middle school some day! Actually, of course, middle school can be wonderful.

Then I met up with a seasoned Dean of Discipline at my school who was known for her strictness and "meanness." One day after school she sat down with me and for hours discussed her ideas on discipline as well as her classroom management techniques. She had an enormous number of excellent suggestions. There were some parts of her presentation that were not suitable for my personality. This is an important point in the art of teaching. Ask for help. Ask for tips. But do not think that you have to take advice "word for word." Listen. Take what is appropriate for you. Find your comfort zone!

The next fourteen years I'll call the "trial and error - get better" years. I taught five classes of junior high school pupils every day. And I learned! I attended workshops, seminars, took courses and networked. I had "good" classes, "bad" classes, nice kids, troubled kids, rough days, easy days, snow days, rain days, large groups and small groups. I developed games, puzzles, survival strategies and management techniques. I rubbed elbows with great teachers, good teachers, poor teachers, great leaders and poor leaders. I tried new ideas and new methods. Some worked and some did not. The "trial and error - get better" years - a fourteen year professional growing experience!

Then, almost suddenly, things started to happen. I decided to go back to school and received a masters degree in educational administration. That was a stimulating and wonderful experience. I applied for and received an "Impact II Developer Grant" from the New York City Board of Education, on which this book is based. That opened up new doors for me.

I then applied for the position of "Dean of Discipline" at my junior high school. Although I had an excellent reputation as a teacher, the administration reluctantly gave me the job. They believed that "students should tremble with fear" when they were sent to the Dean. (My philosophy of "discipline with dignity" was different from theirs. Two years later the administration named me "Teacher of the Year.")

My experience as Dean certainly was the most powerful and influential on me as an educator to that point in my career. I believe it (and what came afterwards) also uniquely qualifies me to write this book (my "Survive Today" book). As Dean, I did just about everything an educator could ever want to do - could ever want to see. I often think of the Christmas movie - "It's A Wonderful Life:" Where would many students be now if I had not touched their lives? And we teachers all could and should feel that way. It is a unique gift available to members of our profession.

First I was put in charge of the pupil cafeteria. This gave me great experience in large group control. General Norman Schwarzkopf (or Dwight Eisenhower) himself might have trouble leading a student lunchroom. We had to feed 300 students in forty-five minutes and assure that all the students were safe and happy. I handled most disciplinary matters for grades six through nine. I had an opportunity to conduct hundreds of one-on-one interviews with children. I learned to listen to their side of the story.

In this role, and later as Assistant Principal at Erasmus High School in Brooklyn and at The HS of Economics and Finance in Manhattan, I had to mediate disputes between parents, pupils, teachers and administrators. I saw evidence of child abuse, drug use, teen pregnancy and suicide. I was a doctor, a referee, a nurse, a psychiatrist, a social worker and a friend. I gave advice. I asked for advice. I learned. I provided crisis intervention for students and staff. I compiled reports, anecdotes and dossiers. I was a detective, a cop and a judge. I was involved with the New York City Police and Transit Police, the Department of Social Services, the courts, the New York City hospitals, and the local neighborhood associations. I learned more about special education and bilingual education. I learned about gangs and violence. I drove fearful students home. I saw students and teachers cry and I cried with them. I learned how to secure a school.

I was active in Parents' Association affairs and learned what concerns parents had in our school. I helped organize events and trips. In other words - I broadened my educational experience tremendously. And this is one very important ingredient in pedagogical improvement: Experience! And by networking with colleagues and observing their techniques, one can radically cut down on the "learning curve," the time it takes to become a very effective classroom management specialist.

I then began presenting my ideas and techniques at many staff development conferences in New York City. This culminated in 1993 in my being invited to three states by the National Council of Math Teachers to present my program at their regional conferences, the highlight of which was an unforgettable three hour mini-course in Columbus, Georgia.

Over the next 5 years, I became a high school math teacher. It provided me with the great opportunity to follow the development and maturation of the junior high school/middle-school student.

In addition, in 1992, I was a finalist in the "Funniest Teacher in New York City" contest held by a local comedy club. That was basically my story as of the initial printing of this book (the "Survive Today" Book). However, here in 2012, so much has happened vis a vis my experiences in education that it has become essential that I add much more to this chapter (and book).

In 1997, I became Assistant Principal at Erasmus High School which will be the topic of another book. Then, from 1997 through 2000, I performed staff and curriculum development for the schools of Brooklyn and Staten

Island and in February 2001, I returned to the classroom to teach math full - time (and become an "in - house" staff development person).

This latter experience provided me with the enormously amazing opportunity to be a "rookie" teacher in a school (but a "special" rookie - one possessing 27 years of experience) with the opportunity to perform "battle duty."

Now that you know more about me, I hope that it will help you to understand much of the program that will be presented in the pages that follow. This sentence is approximately where (in terms of material) the first edition (of "Just Let Me Survive Today") ended in 1995.

When this book had its first printing, I had been at Lincoln HS for three years. Let me pick up now at the remainder of my career at Lincoln and move onto this next phase of my experiences (as introduced above).

At Lincoln High School, I spent five glorious years in my first (non summer) High School experience. I served as my union's "Chapter Leader" - this involved me in lots of day to day conflicts between teachers and administrators. It also gave me the experience that helped teach me how to settle disagreements between people with (at times greatly) differing viewpoints on usually quite controversial and/or emotionally - charged issues.

This "expertise" helped sharpen my skills in settling disputes between pupils who often were involved in remarkably similar interpersonal disputes, in working with gang members and in other potentially volatile situations. At the time I began teaching at Lincoln, my great chairman, Harold Kornblum, encouraged me to get involved in teaching a most rigorous course - Advanced Placement Calculus. Since I hadn't taken this class since college, it motivated me to learn massive amounts of very complicated material and quickly teach it to a group of 25 very gifted children, who would challenge me with major league questions.

This occurrence was yet another wonderful "growing" experience in my career. It helped me learn how to investigate, prepare and refine unfamiliar curricula - and adapt it to the demands of a most challenging and gifted group of youngsters. It helped put me "in the shoes" of my target population and helped me handle quite a stressful situation.

The graphing calculator was another major new ingredient - I had never used it before, and its mastery was required on the AP Calculus Exam. Many of my pupils, growing up in the computer age, were extremely adept with this technology and I even took "lessons" (during my lunch period) from some of them. It was a year of extremely hard work - preparing very intricate material for "double" periods totaling 90 minutes per day.

Some of the brighter pupils constantly challenged me, often "showing off" by trying to "show me up." Often I needed to prepare into the "wee hours" of the night for these gambits by day. There were major rewards however, when large percentages of my class fared exceedingly well on the most challenging AP exam. It also reinforced my belief in always taking on new challenges - no matter how intimidating or threatening. These experiences are golden in trying to mold one's character and in making one a much better educator. I also encourage all of my pupils and colleagues to constantly take on new challenges and to always "go for it."

At Lincoln HS I had a wonderful position. I was teaching some wonderful children in calculus class and in Algebra and served as the union representative for my school. Still, I left. Over the summer of 1997, I had received a call from the Principal of a really tough inner city High School in Brooklyn NY called Erasmus Hall High School. This school had lots of problems - dropouts, poor academic results, gangs, fighting - you name it. I was asked to become the Assistant Principal in charge of Guidance, Security and Math. I decided to take this (potentially) very stressful job. It was in keeping with my philosophy of "go for it." It would give me 30 years of experience in one year - and it did!!

As Assistant Principal of Guidance, on a daily basis I dealt with an almost constant stream of serious disciplinary situations - gang involvement, fights, and security issues of quite an intense level. I learned so much that year - about graduation requirements, transcripts, family problems, etc. I dealt with police, hospitals, family courts, probation officers. I learned to deal with very hardcore tough disciplinary cases. It helped me to become a better classroom and school wide disciplinarian. I ran a lunchroom in which 800 pupils dined at one time in one (quite large) room. This experience taught me that I could handle almost anything.

There were challenging decisions daily that had to be made one after another. In fact, there were so many that they became "easy" to deal with. It sharpened my decision - making abilities - under stress.

The pupils and teachers loved me, trusted me, and respected me. I gave all the same respect and kindness. But you know what? After a while, it became a bit depressing to deal day after day with discipline problems and crime related issues. I longed to return to more academically oriented pursuits. That's when the next call came. After working nineteen years at the same school, I was about to accept my fourth new job in seven years. Change was good for me

- it kept my world exciting and my mind and soul growing quite positively. I suggest it for everyone from time to time. The reading of "Who Moved My Cheese?" encouraged me!

That call came in late spring 1998. Would you like to assume the exciting role of Math Staff and Curriculum Development Specialist for most of the High Schools in Brooklyn and Staten Island NY? You would be training teachers in methods of teaching math to all levels of students, you'd be developing curriculum, giving hundreds of workshops, attending just as many, learning about cutting edge studies on brain research, cooperative learning strategies, among many other stimulating items; you'd be traveling city-wide, state-wide, country-wide, meeting hundreds of different people and lots of teachers and administrators; you'd be able to write, create - learn all about the latest methods of monitoring students and study techniques. Every day you will wake up and you'll be like a kid in a candy store of educational opportunity. You bet I'll accept!

This position led to nearly three years of further personal and professional growth. But once again I was removed from actual classroom involvement. One can begin to drift and become "out of touch." In New York City at the time (about 2000-2001) there were large groups of students who were failing the HS "exit" exam (the "Regents" exam), an exam required for graduation. The curriculum folks developed a unique idea. They would send those (mostly) seniors to summer school from July 1 through August 17, and tailor 3 hour intensive math class instruction for them every day.

The thinking was that these "super sized" (time wise) classes might provide the necessary blitz of knowledge. Most teachers felt it a crazy idea to take these kids who had failed algebra numerous times (and in many cases were severe behavior problems) and subject them (and their teacher) to three hours of continuous instruction. I thought so too but nothing else had worked. A problem though: No one really wanted to teach the class or, for that matter, was trained or equipped to do so. I was asked to write a training manual for this class, for there would be perhaps forty or so of these classes city wide.

In preparing the manual I literally had to "walk through" the three hour lesson 30 times (for 30 days) in order to cover the entire year's material. I realized that teaching this class would be enormously challenging and truly doubted its success. But, I also became quite excited thinking that I might perhaps pilot teach this class. Yes! How could I write an accurate roadmap for other teachers if I did not instruct this class and play with my ideas in actual practice? So I did. During the summers of 2000 and 2001, I taught this 7 week summer course to seniors who needed to pass this algebra exam to graduate. And how stimulating and rewarding it was!! I was back in the classroom under pressure to succeed and to succeed with pupils who had failed miserably to this point.

Mostly, I called upon my 30 years of educational experience - the ideas contained in this book. I followed chapter and verse: "Just Let Me Survive Today!" I used my techniques of human relations. I also had pupils play math games, win prizes, do targeted practice exercises and drill. I had a student teacher for the first time in 30 years - an enthusiastic college student about to become a teacher himself who helped enormously and who related to my pupils very effectively. (Always volunteer to get a student teacher if the possibility arises).

However, recall now that I had not been in the classroom much for the past four years. I'd been an administrator and staff and curriculum developer. But I had learned so much in those last four years and now was the time to bring all this learning to the classroom.

I'd learned about the latest ideas from the world of "brain research." I knew now that pupil understanding could be even more enhanced by cooperative learning - by working together in small groups and helping one another. The kids needed study skills strategies. I created many mnemonics - and other little tricks to help them memorize necessary formulas and facts. Most pupils loved to dance and listen to music so we put many of the mathematical formulas "to music" and created dance steps to make the learning more fun and much more effective. An example of the "Dance Manual" appears in Figures 40 - 42 (of the "Survive" Book).

The 3 hour classes went by so quickly. Each daily session was broken up into various parts - first a lecture, then a math game. We followed this by a cooperative learning session, an open-book quiz, some dancing and singing, another game, another mini-lecture, and wrapped it up by using a "math cheer," a quiz or a massive bingo math review game. Every day was a Broadway Extravaganza. In addition, we used the USA Today to link the math to "real-world" events and practices.

We also injected much from the world of technology - using the internet to help us develop lesson strategies and targeted math recreation. Technology in the form of calculators (scientific and graphing) was introduced and taught at critical junctures to help enhance pupil understanding. I received a grant on the use of technology in the classroom.

Along the lines of study strategies, pupils were taught how to take notes while reading and while in class and how to organize these notes so that they could become effective tools for learning. Many other study skills strategies were implemented, which is the subject of an upcoming book.

All pupils (including special education) enhanced their methods of study by leaps and bounds. Most pupils previously had no conception of any of this studying methodology. Most pupils, I find, really want to do well. However, they often lack the study skills that will ensure the best chance for success.

Finally, August 17th and the exit exam (the NY State "Regents") day had arrived. Amazingly, over 70% of the class (of about 36 pupils) passed the exam. Many others came very close. A "miracle" had occurred in Brooklyn. I was onto something - big. I have since repeated this summertime model (similar) at Columbia HS in Maplewood.

I spent 6 more months as a staff developer, bringing enhanced enthusiasm and realism to my presentations. I had actually been successful. Yes, "all students can learn," a phrase I had repeated (yet never truly believed) for years. I now truly believed it and this was an amazing revelation for me. My workshops became much more exciting as I enthusiastically delivered presentations that were now truly ingrained in my heart and soul.

By the spring of 2001 I had succumbed to the teaching "bug" completely. I needed to be in the classroom full time to experiment and practice with my strategies. The classroom would become my laboratory where I would experiment and practice my craft - my art. In addition, it seemed that teachers often had little time in their busy and stressful days to sit and hear lectures from a non - practicing staff developer (like myself) who had a "cushy" "district office" job (as "in house" teachers often viewed it), never getting his hands dirty in the everyday teaching grind. I needed to be among them once again. Additionally, I would have more time to converse with colleagues and they would pay much more attention to one (i.e., me) going through the same day - to - day stresses!

So, in February, 2001, I returned to the classroom full time - not only in summertime. The site was Automotive HS, a (nearly) all boys vocational school in Brooklyn, NY - a school on the verge of "shut down" due to poor academic results - a school in "redesign" with one last chance to reverse its fortunes.

There was a new principal and a veteran (very competent - dedicated) Assistant Principal of Mathematics and Science (who would later become a Principal herself). Yes, I was back in the classroom once again in quite a difficult inner city school. But you know what? I loved it! I brought those same wonderful summer school strategies to "Auto." The kids loved the methods and a school that most teachers avoided at any cost, to me, was heaven.

What I saw was a needy student population with a group of truly dedicated and caring teachers trying to reverse a history of failure and coming up against all sorts of difficult odds - lack of money, budget cuts, and really tough students mostly used to failure. Yet the teachers, through meeting after meeting, idea after idea and dedication and spirit like I had not seen (too often) before, gradually were piecing the school back together into a hopeful place with lots of potential.

For me, the term gave another challenging opportunity to work through my strategies with yet more students, who most had "written off." Even more challenging was that this time many were not seniors so their backs were not "up against the wall." Motivation and spirit were needed much more in this school. In addition, as mentioned, I had the amazingly unique opportunity to be treated like a rookie teacher - yet one with 30 years or so of vast educational experience. It gave me the chance (using my experience and insight) to lay back and gradually observe the inner workings (both positive and negative) of a school and to try and contribute ideas that might help the school turn the corner and succeed more effectively. This term's experience certainly showed me that a united faculty dedicated to improving their lot and that of their pupils certainly can help to improve conditions for all and make it a more hopeful and positive place in which to work.

One major example was a union created "Teacher Center" at Automotive. It was a huge room made for teachers only. Here teachers could go, before, after, and during school, and do any lesson planning, test grading, eating, relaxing and using the excellent and available duplicating facilities. They could relax and "schmooze," use the phone, and enjoy coffee and snacks any time of day. They could observe workshops or watch TV. The great asset however, was that this large and well - staffed and maintained (by a union member whose sole job was to manage this room and provide major emotional and academic support for teachers) room provided a major oasis for staff during their busy and stressful day. No school I'd been in before or since had this truly amazing set up! It helped make a hugely stressful situation much more palatable. It was heaven is what it was.

My Automotive period was quite challenging and enlightening. The point of the "Teacher Center anecdote" is that teachers need to push to establish this kind of atmosphere - where they can relax, unwind and prepare for their classes in other than the often traditional cramped and demoralizing situation.

The summer of 2001 took me back for another successful summer school tour, again with those three hour classes. And, the numbers were quite positive, reflecting further academic success. My system had now proven the test of time.

Automotive High School made it six different highly unique positions over a nine year time period. As mentioned, varying positions and jobs like this helped me stay focused and full of excitement and spirit.

Then in late August 2001, I received yet another call. Would I like to become Assistant Principal (again) of Math, Science and Economics and Finance - at the High School of Economics and Finance in downtown Manhattan - only one block from the World Trade Center? Well, it would again take me "out of the classroom" (except for teaching one calculus class) and into the arms of administration. It was a school with ten floors located in an office building in the heart of the financial district of New York City. It had major involvement with some of the largest financial institutions in the world. It was New York City - The Big Apple!! After 29 years in education I had finally made it to (near) Broadway - full time. Of course I would accept - it was a wonderful opportunity to become part of a cutting edge and potentially enormous growth situation.

After only a few days on this most challenging and stimulating job, I was having a conversation with my principal when we heard a "BOOM" outside. The building shook. I immediately thought - "bomb." As it turned out, it was about 9 AM, and it was 9/11/01, and we were at 100 Trinity Place - right across the street from the "Twin Towers." You know much of the rest - or do you?? We had over 800 pupils in our building. We were not permitted to evacuate as there was falling debris and potential disaster on the street. We felt new respect for our well - run fire/shelter drills as most kept calm amid a background of horrible reports that we were beginning to hear.

This is yet another aspect of education. Amid crises and even disaster we must model calm leadership to help our children cope. After the second plane hit the tower, we were given orders to evacuate. We marched our 800 pupils and staff down up to ten stairwells and out of the building. There was falling debris (and even bodies) as we wound our way through the streets of (a fairly unfamiliar area for me) lower NYC.

We all gathered near the "Bowling Green" subway station when suddenly the first tower began to (unbelievably) collapse. It sent a hurricane of swirling debris right in our direction (or, basically every direction). We all took off.

It was terrifying as we became separated and eventually were covered with little particles of eye and face burning "dust." Which way to run? Is everyone OK? Will we live? Will we go blind as our eyes closed to small slits as the unthinkable unfolded? Well, the remaining hours and even days can serve as the material for another book down the road.

It turns out, we all miraculously survived - much of it due to the leadership and bravery under pressure exhibited by our staff and students. We could not return to our damaged school building for over seven months. During this period I again received an education in leadership and survival. See figure 44 (in the "Survive Today" book) for further data on this incident.

We had to share a building with Norman Thomas High School, located in midtown Manhattan. The big problem was that we had to wait to begin our school day until their shortened day had ended. This resulted for us in a quite difficult curtailed school day (for nearly seven months) that began about 1:30 PM and ended at approximately 6 PM.

When we finally resumed classes a couple of days after 9/11 at our new site, we began with almost no textbooks (everything was back at our original site), hardly any duplicating facilities - and the school year was still only in its extreme early stages. It turned out to be an unbelievably challenging year, to put it quite mildly. We received millions of dollars in grants and were the subject of TV and radio shows, newspaper articles and honors. The psychological effects were certainly, in some cases, major. But we did all pull together like a family that had survived a horrible situation - and we emerged as a strong team. We did give 110% and had an amazing year, doing the best that could be expected of anyone in that situation.

I received a "crash course" in administration. I learned, under extreme pressure, how to deal with emergencies, choose and order textbooks (thousands of them), and help to program a school. From what appeared to be an overwhelmingly impossible situation we turned things around, stabilized them and moved forward, trying to salvage an entire school year. And we succeeded! Of course, in cases as this (in education and in life), we emerged truly stronger for having been through this horror. And so it is as a teacher - rookie or veteran - there will be minor and, at times, major ups and downs. One must remain positive, focused, dedicated, professional, and resilient and, above all, <u>one must persevere!!</u> You will emerge a stronger teacher, a better teacher, a better person. And your pupils will emerge better prepared to face the challenges that life has to offer.

Another stressful year was spent as an administrator rather successfully patching together a broken situation. I needed to get out of NY City (Manhattan) at this point. I had moved to Millburn, New Jersey (big commute from here to NYC) and seized on the opportunity to once again return to teaching full time. I secured a position as a math teacher in a school much closer to my new home - Port Richmond HS in Staten Island, NY.

It was now fall of 2002. Every single one of my 130 pupils had failed math the previous year and were "repeaters." They came with the usual cartload of personal, academic and emotional problems. It was time for me once again to rise to the challenge. I was, as mentioned, now in Staten Island NY, one of the outer boroughs of New York City. So, I spent these final two years of my NYC career at Port Richmond HS in Staten Island - a school with a long history - built many decades ago. The pupils were every bit as challenging as those I struggled with back in September of 1973. Although "the times they have been a - changing," the basic nature of the child has not. Kids still responded very well to fun, games, prizes, and stimulating lessons. But most of all, they responded well to positive, respectful treatment, much of which they had never had previously.

Well again I pulled together my ever - growing experiences as an educator to find my way with yet another crop of new students, new colleagues and new bosses. The challenge continues. I seem to go on and on having more fun and pleasure the further I go.

On August 6, 2004, I officially retired from the NYC Public School System after over 32 years. And guess what? I am now about to begin the ninth year in my "second career" out here in my now home state of New Jersey. In 2004, I had accepted a new position as a math teacher at Columbia HS in Maplewood NJ. I have been teaching, among other subjects, AP Calculus. I recently completed a one week training session on the techniques of teaching this most rigorous class. As always, teachers must "keep current" as to the latest strategies of the given subject at hand.

Now here we are in February 2013 as I am now, as mentioned, into my ninth wonderful year at Columbia HS. It has been a wonderful experience experimenting with all the practices I had been using for my 32 years in NYC.

It seems that every year I am faced with a new crop of pupils and challenges.

Good luck to all of you. I hope you all have as wonderful, exciting and challenging a career in education as I've had - and continue to have!! Always remain positive and optimistic about the possibilities. They are truly endless!!

FIGURE TWO

MY PHILOSOPHY OF EDUCATION

Any program must begin with a basic philosophy. Of course, learning the subject matter is of great importance. However, those often-neglected affective (emotional) aspects of education are critical, and of utmost urgency. They are a big priority. I wrote a book called: "High Caliber Kids" - which is a collection of sports stories that aim to teach values through sports. In the introduction, I wrote:

"Our planet has at times been on the brink of nuclear disaster. The subject matter of values, getting along with others and all other aspects of trait and character development are of extreme timeliness. If this subject matter is not employed today, we may not reach tomorrow. Through sports, we can teach the appreciation of basic values, as well as the responsibilities we all have as members of society."

Herein lies the key to my educational philosophy. We must teach students how to get along with and respect one another. We must help to build their self-confidence and self-esteem. We must teach them how to socialize. Every aspect of good human relations must be illustrated to our pupils. We want them to enjoy learning, perhaps even to love their subjects, and to have fun in school. We need for our children to learn how to communicate more effectively and to be able to express themselves in their lives. Finally, of course, are the cognitive aspects of skill development.

In applying to become a school administrator in New York City, I was required to fill out an application over eight pages long. One question was to explain my philosophy of education. I will reprint it here, because it further summarizes much of what I want you to know about me:

"I have worked as a counselor for fifteen years in a summer camp run by a director with a truly idealistic vision of society "the way it ought to be." This, in combination with my own substantial professional and personal growth, has served to inject in me a spirit and optimism that almost anything is possible - a feeling which I hope to convey to all those with whom I come in contact.

In my life experiences I have found that certain traits are very important. Among them are kindness, consideration for the rights and property of others, politeness, responsibility, dependability, loyalty and integrity. I believe the children are our future and we are entrusted with most important work.

By using our knowledge, experience and insight, we must help all of those we touch become better for having known us. We must teach, however, that change requires time, patience and hard work. We must stress honesty and not allow for manipulative behavior.

We must experiment and investigate to discover the needs of our students. Once accomplished, we must vary our instructional strategies and the nature of our relationships with our students depending on the unique situation at hand. We must set up our schools so that all involved have high probability of having frequent "peak" experiences. Only when pupils are very interested in and excited about the subject matter, either for practical or spiritual reasons, can we expect them to experience these wonderful feelings.

I am seeking this position because I feel that my philosophy, as explained, combined with my vast educational experience, optimism, great enthusiasm and love for children, will combine to result in a highly positive and effective outcome for all involved."

All the various components of my teaching and SAT/ACT program are permeated by the spirit living within my educational philosophy.

FIGURE THREE

THE SAT/ACT CIRCLE OF SUCCESS

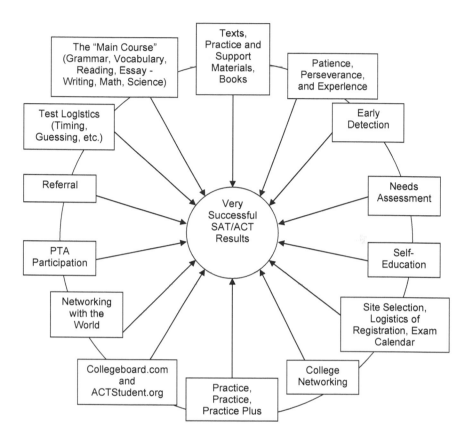

FIGURE FOUR

THE PARENTING CIRCLE OF SUCCESS

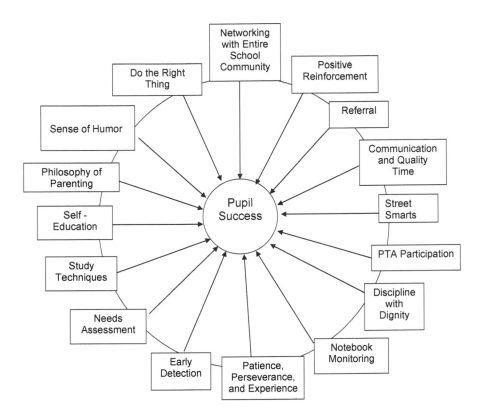

Made in the USA
Lexington, KY
28 September 2014